JAZZ MOSAIC

Jazz Activities for the Early Childhood Classroom

Louise Rogers & Susan Milligan

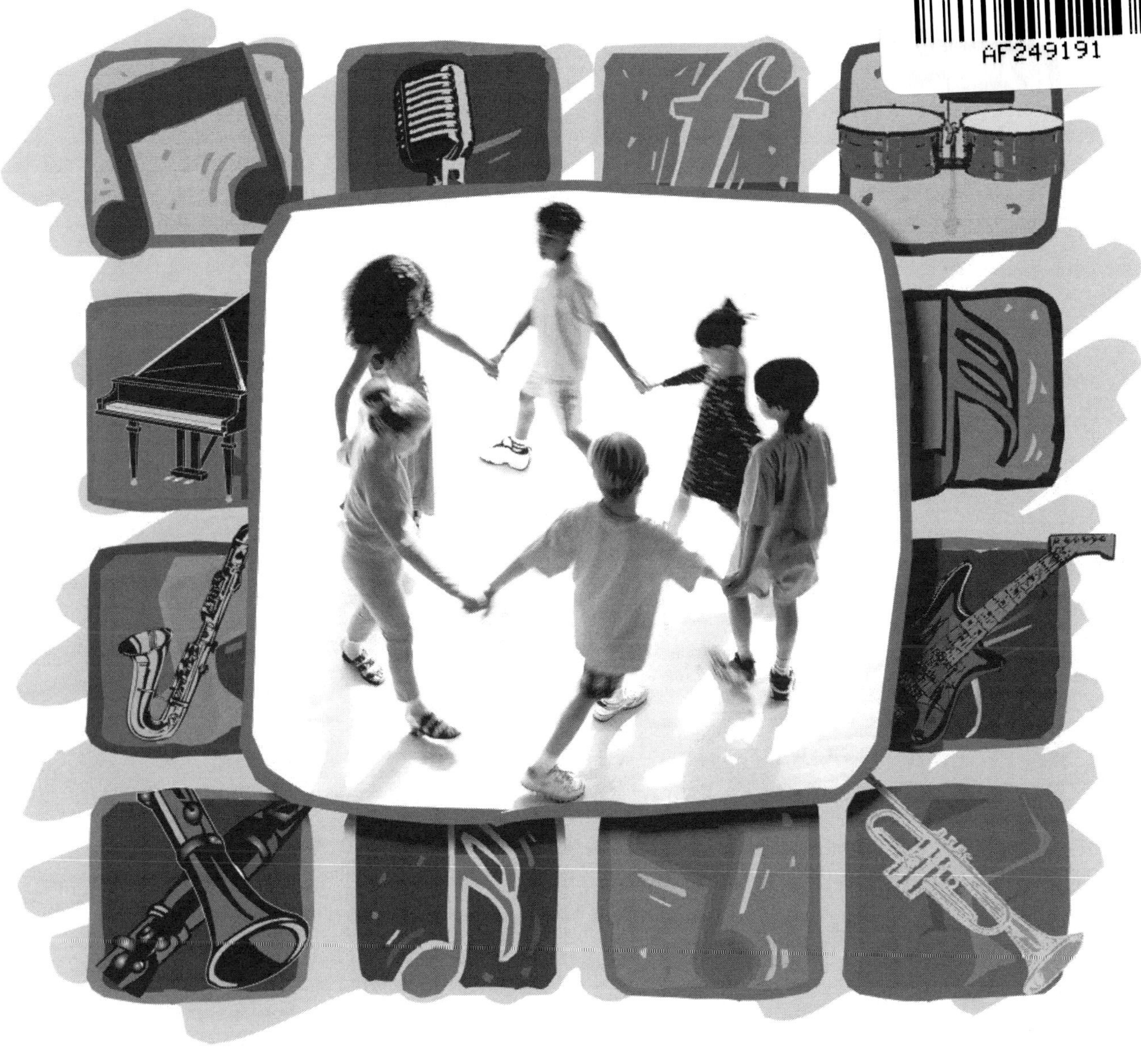

Alfred Music Publishing Co., Inc.
16320 Roscoe Blvd., Suite 100
P.O. Box 10003
Van Nuys, CA 91410-0003

Alfred

alfred.com

Contents

Introduction

Jazz Mosaic helps to bring the joy of music into your classroom every day through a variety of jazz-related, age-appropriate, play-centered lessons that can be easily integrated into your existing curriculum. These activities are appropriate for children from pre-school through third grade.

Research now shows what teachers of young children have always felt to be true. Music in the daily lives of children has a huge impact on their well-being and development. Being part of a meaningful, musical experience provides a child with an outlet for creative expression and invokes a wonderful feeling of unity and achievement.

The *National Association for Music Education* policy on music in the daily lives of children includes this statement:

> Music is a natural and important part of young children's growth and development. Early interaction with music positively affects the quality of all children's lives. Successful experiences in music help all children bond emotionally and intellectually with others through creative expression in song, rhythmic movement, and listening experiences. Music in early childhood creates a foundation upon which future music learning is built. These experiences should be integrated within the daily routine and play of children. In this way, enduring attitudes regarding the joy of music making and sharing are developed.

> Music education for young children involves a developmentally appropriate program of singing, moving, listening, creating, playing instruments, and responding to visual and verbal representations of sound. The content of such a program should represent music of various cultures in time and place. Time should be made available during the day for activities in which music is the primary focus of attention for its own value. It may also serve as a means for teachers to facilitate the accomplishment of nonmusical goals. Musical experiences should be play-based.

Jazz Mosaic provides a broad range of enjoyable and educational activities from which to choose for both classroom and music teachers.

What is Jazz?

Simply put, jazz is an integration of African and European music.

In New Orleans, African slaves would gather at Congo Square. Here the community came together in song, dance, and drumming. The rhythmic component of African music with its improvisational nature, chanting, and call and response songs were among the first distinguishing characteristics of jazz.

The more structured European musical influence of the Creoles blended with the music of the African slaves in New Orleans. Eventually, a new music evolved into what we now know as jazz. The key elements of jazz are swing, syncopation, blues and improvisation which includes scat singing. These elements are discussed in detail later in this chapter under *Elements of Jazz*.

Jazz really began to take shape in the 1920s. Swing bands like Benny Goodman's, vocalists like Ella Fitzgerald, and instrumentalists like Louis Armstrong helped to make jazz the popular music of the 1930s and 1940s.

Why Jazz?

Jazz is imaginative.	*Jazz is syncopated.*
Jazz is spontaneous.	Jazz swings.
Jazz is improvisational.	*Jazz is creative.*
Jazz is play-centered.	Jazz is personal.
Jazz is easily accessible.	*Jazz is social.*
Jazz is experimental.	Jazz helps foster language development.
Jazz is multi-cultural.	

Jazz is fun!

"It was when I realized I could make mistakes, that I knew I was on to something."
Ornette Coleman

Jazz is easily accessible to music teachers, classroom teachers and children. ***Jazz Mosaic*** provides lesson plans for teachers of all abilities. The playfulness of jazz makes it ideal, not only for music class, but for the early childhood classroom as well. Jazz is a play-centered approach to music and is a developmentally appropriate learning style for young children. Participating in jazz related activities is the perfect outlet for children to express themselves musically, playfully and creatively.

As a music teacher or classroom teacher, you will not have to take time away from skill-building in other areas. Listening skills, creative expression, musicianship, respect and camaraderie develop as the children practice and learn together in this playful environment. Children also learn literacy, math, small and large motor skills, visual arts, and social studies while they are having fun with jazz.

Jazz is an experimental, highly creative art form. When a child improvises musically, he or she is allowed the freedom to experiment and is encouraged to be imaginative, spontaneous, and playful within the structure of the music or activity. Jazz opens the door to higher level thinking: decision making, problem solving, imagining, and realizing new ideas.

Elements of Jazz 

Call and Response

The call and response method is an integral part of jazz. Call and response echoes back to African work songs, the foundation on which jazz was built. A melody was sung, followed by a response. It is also a tried and true teaching method which all teachers will recognize —the teacher says a new word, states a rhythm, or sings a melody and the children repeat it or echo it back. The call and response method allows young children to actively participate in learning, making it a highly effective teaching method. It helps to build important communication and social skills such as listening to others and waiting for your turn to speak.

Scat Language and Improvisation

After the melody is introduced or "stated" at the beginning of a piece, there is usually an element of improvisation involved while singing or playing an instrument. Within the structure of the piece, the musicians create a "new" melody and/or rhythm in place of the original one.

Scat is a jazz language used by singers to try to make their voices sound like musical instruments. The singer sings made-up word-sounds and improvises a melody that "fits" with the chords of the music.

A typical scat phrase may sound like: *Buh – doo – buh – doo - bah* or *Reedy - bop Reedy - bop* or *Dwee – ah – doo – bop*. When you are scatting you are playing with sounds, which is an age-appropriate literacy and music activity for young children. It's also a lot of fun for teachers.

Rhythm

Music is organized sound as opposed to noise. It is important for children to understand that banging randomly on a drum is not making music. Rhythm is a strong regular repeated pattern of sound. Rhythm is basic to music. The underlying organization of jazz music is its rhythm.

We use percussion instruments in early childhood classrooms so that children can find the rhythm and keep the beat of live and recorded music. Math readiness skills, such as patterning and fractions, can be learned by playing and practicing rhythms.

Jazz Mosaic introduces children to several different rhythms including swing and syncopation. They will *hear* the rhythms in the songs and in the underlying bass accompaniments and they will *feel* the rhythms as they move their bodies in time to the music. These rhythms occur naturally and children will internalize the rhythms as they play with them. (See the Appendix for more information about rhythm.)

Movement

Jazz music was the pop music of the early to mid 20th Century. People danced when they heard jazz. Popular dances of the time were the Charleston, Lindy-Hop, Jitterbug, and Swing. Jazz musicians feel the pulse and movement of their music and many of them love to dance. Young children love to move to the rhythms of jazz, too, making it a great way to involve them in music everyday. Kids might enjoy watching video clips of the various dances. Such videos can be found on-line.

The Blues

Without the blues, we wouldn't have jazz. The blues originated many years ago but really began to take form in the nineteenth century. Filled with emotion, this rich form combining music and storytelling began with the work songs of African slaves. They sang the blues when they were sad to make them feel better and/or to tell a story.

Jazz Greats

There have been and continue to be many wonderful jazz musicians. *Jazz Mosaic* introduces and highlights a handful of them—Ella Fitzgerald, Charlie Parker, Miles Davis, Louis Armstrong, Benny Goodman, Duke Ellington, Tito Puente, and Taj Majal. It is important for children to understand that real men and women from many different cultures created the recorded music they enjoy listening to today. In addition, we have highlighted poet Eve Merriam, whose poetry is explored via jazz.

Jazz Festival

A jazz festival is a wonderful way to celebrate the arts with your community. In Chapter 10 of this book, we outline the steps that help you plan a successful event. *Jazz Mosaic* has all the information you need to know in order to have a successful festival in your school.

How to Use This Book

Music teachers and classroom teachers can use this guide to provide daily music experiences for their children. The improvisational nature of jazz allows it to be used successfully in many settings. This book offers:

- Lesson ideas which can be easily incorporated into any curriculum.
- A menu of ideas from which teachers can choose.
- Activities for both small and large groups.
- Easy to follow music lesson plans
- Age-appropriate activities for both early childhood and early elementary classrooms.
- Flexible activities for children with special needs.
- Information in the Appendix to help teachers choose appropriate supplemental music and literature for their classrooms.

Implemented cover-to-cover, **Jazz Mosaic** provides a year-long music curriculum.

Chapter 1

Scatting — Ella Fitzgerald

"The only thing better than singing is more singing."
attributed to Ella Fitzgerald

JAZZ GREAT—Ella Fitzgerald (1917–1996)

Ella Fitzgerald was born in Newport News, Virginia on April 25, 1917. Shortly after her birth her family moved to Yonkers, New York. Ella was an excellent student and enjoyed school. But what Ella loved to do most was to dance and sing. She often danced on the sidewalk for her friends. Ella imagined that the sidewalk was her stage.

On November 21, 1934, at the age of 17, Ella entered a talent contest at the Apollo Theater in Harlem, New York. She had wanted to dance at the talent contest. However, when Ella arrived at the theater, she was discouraged. All of the other dancers were dressed quite stylishly and she was embarrassed by her appearance. She was wearing old clothes that had been handed down to her. So, at the last minute she changed her mind and decided to sing. It was a good decision. The crowd loved her and she won first prize that night at the Apollo Theater Talent Contest! Ella's first big hit was "A Tisket, A Tasket" with the Chick Webb Orchestra.

Ella went on to become one of the world's most famous jazz singers. She sold over 40 million albums and won 13 Grammy awards. One of her most famous songs was "Take the A Train."

Ella was well-known for her vocal improvisations. She learned how to make her voice sound like an instrument by using made up word-sounds. We call this scatting. In fact, Ella was known as the "Queen of Scat."

One of Ella's biggest idols was Louis Armstrong who is often credited with having invented scat. Both Louis and Ella influenced many other singers. For more on Louis Armstrong, go to Chapter 4. For a list of other scat singers, please go to the Appendix.

Ella Fitzgerald Teaching Suggestions

Tell the class a little bit about Ella Fitzgerald. Be sure to mention:

- Ella was born in Virginia but grew up Yonkers, New York.

- She loved to dance and sing and often pretended that the sidewalk was her stage.

- On November 21, 1934, at the age of 17, Ella won a talent contest at the Apollo Theater in Harlem, New York. She had planned on dancing but was intimidated by the stylish clothing of the other dancers and at the last minute, decided to sing instead.

- Her first big hit was "A Tisket, A Tasket" with the Chick Webb Orchestra.

- "Take the A Train" was one of her biggest hits.

- She was well known for her scatting (vocal improvisation).

Note to Teachers: Children are introduced to Ella Fitzgerald's love of scatting and her unforgettable voice through the simple poem below. It references the "A" train, a famous subway in New York City. The "A" Train travels through Harlem, home to the Apollo Theater where Ella entered the talent contest. Ella undoubtedly rode this train.

The Poem

Materials needed

- ***Ella Fitzgerald Sang Bop Boo Day,*** *Track #3 on CD.*
- Words to the poem on the CD.

  Ella Fitzgerald sang bop boo day.
  Her Beboppin' voice is here to stay.
  She bopped along the track on a train called A,
  And Ella Fitzgerald Sang Bop Boo day.

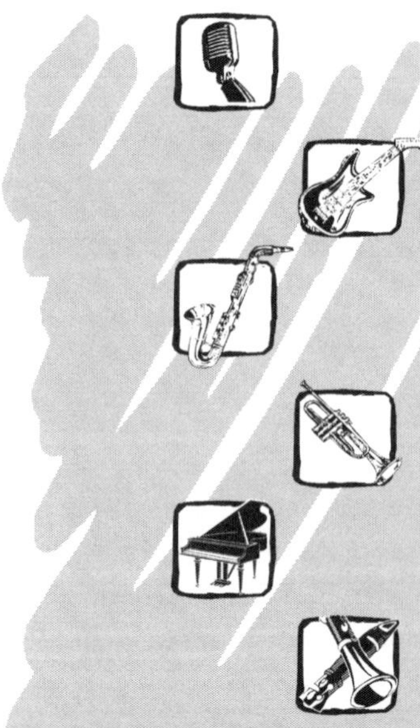

Procedure

- Listen to Track #3 with the children.
- Recite the entire poem and have children echo back line by line.

  Teacher: Ella Fitzgerald sang bop boo day

  Class: Ella Fitzgerald sang bop boo day

  Teacher: Her beboppin' voice is here to stay

  Class: Her beboppin' voice is here to stay

  Teacher: She bopped along the track on a train called A

  Class: She bopped along the track on a train called A

  Teacher: And Ella Fitzgerald sang bop boo day

  Class: And Ella Fitzgerald sang bop boo day

Ella Fitzgerald Sang Bop Boo Day

Lousie Rogers

Adding the Scat Section

Scat: "Scat" is a jazz language used by vocalists when trying to make their voices sound like instruments. The singer sings made-up words and a made-up melody that "fit" or sound good over the chords of the piece. When you are scatting you are playing with sounds, which is an age appropriate literacy and music activity for young children and a whole lot of fun.

Whether you are singing or speaking your scat phrases, we encourage you to explore your voice and have fun! Adding some of the following musical elements will help to make your scat phrases more interesting and diverse:

- Dynamics—the loudness or softness of your voice.

- Crescendos—allowing your voice to slowly get louder.

- Decrescendos—allowing your voice to slowly get softer.

- Slides—sliding your voice from one note to another.

- Rests—allowing pauses in your scat phrases.

- Inflection—changing the tone or pitch of your voice while either speaking or singing. This happens naturally as we speak. We do not speak in a monotone. For example, when we ask a question, our voice usually goes up in pitch at the end of the sentence.

- High voice and low voice—changing out of your natural register. How high can you go? How low can you go? Experiment.

- Rhythmic Diversity—long words and short words.

- Patterns—creating rhythmic and or melodic patterns.

- Syncopation—a syncopated rhythm is one that delivers an element of rhythmic surprise.

Note: In jazz, we use a lot of syncopated rhythms. Our bodies are accustomed to feeling the steady pulse of the music we commonly listen to. A syncopated rhythm surprises us because it comes "off the beat." For example, "Bop booo day" becomes "Bop boo day," shortening the "booo" to "boo." Below are a few examples. The X marks the syncopated rhythms. The first measure is not syncopated.

Syncopation

Talking Scats

The scat section is a lot of fun! If you are not comfortable singing, you can make up a spoken scat.

You can teach scat phrases to the students in the same manner as the poem was taught—by having the class be your echo. Have fun creating your own. The examples below will give you some ideas to get you started.

Teacher: Bop boo bop

Class: Bop boo bop

Teacher: "Beedle deedle dop

Class: Beedle deedle dop"

Teacher: Skee bah doo bop

Class: Skee bah doo bop

Teacher: Bid-dl-ee-Did-dl-ee-dop

Class: Bid-dl-ee-Did-dl-ee-dop

Teacher: Bay bah doo bop

Class: Bay bah doo bop!

Teacher: Hoooooo-bop

Class: Hoooooo-bop

Singing Scats

Materials Needed (one of the below will do):

- a pitch-pipe

- a piano

- a keyboard

- a xylophone

- a glockenspiel

Procedure

- If you are comfortable singing the scat phrases, you will need to establish a key or a tonality to make it musical. A child's voice is usually higher than an adult's voice. The written music below is in the key of C major which is a good key for children.

Ella Fitzgerald Sang Bop Boo Day

Lousie Rogers

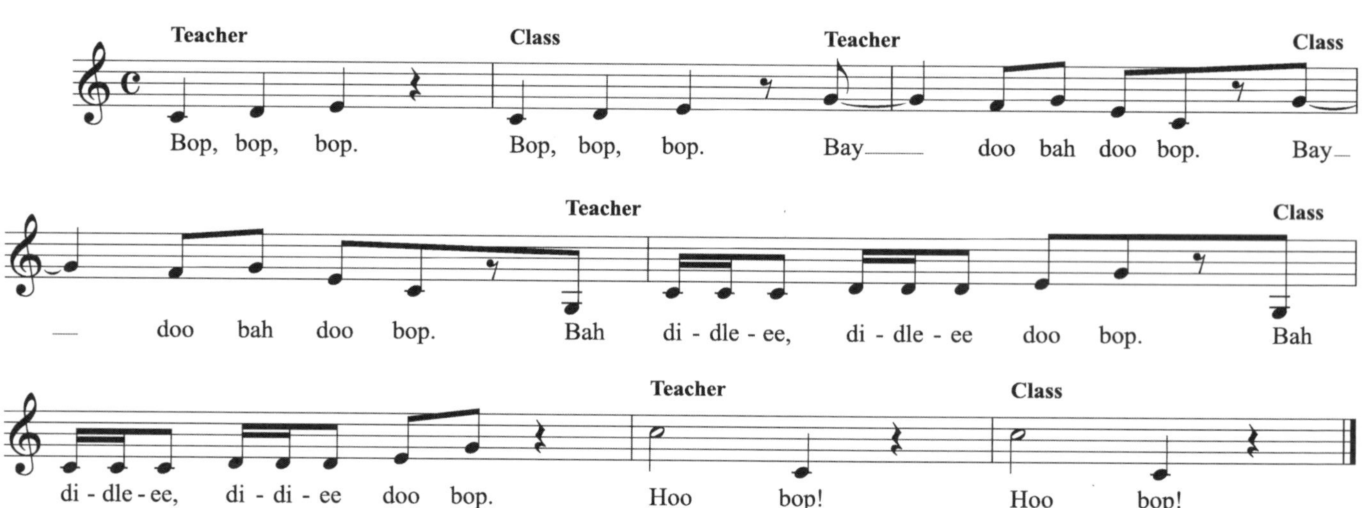

To establish the key of C, play a C and a G on the instrument of your choice.

- Choose from the sample scat phrases or create your own original scat phrases for students to echo back.

- Start with simple phrases.

- As the students become more comfortable with scatting, progress to scat phrases that are more challenging.

- Encourage children to take turns being the scat leader. The rest of the class echoes the leader's phrases.

Scatting Extensions

As the class becomes more comfortable scatting, they will be able to create their own scat phrases.

- Sitting in a circle, tell the class that they will each have a turn to scat.

- After each scat, the class chants together the phrase "Ella Fitzgerald sang bop boo day." Below is a melody so that you can sing the chant if you wish.

- Encourage children to sing their scat phrases.

Ella Chant

Lousie Rogers

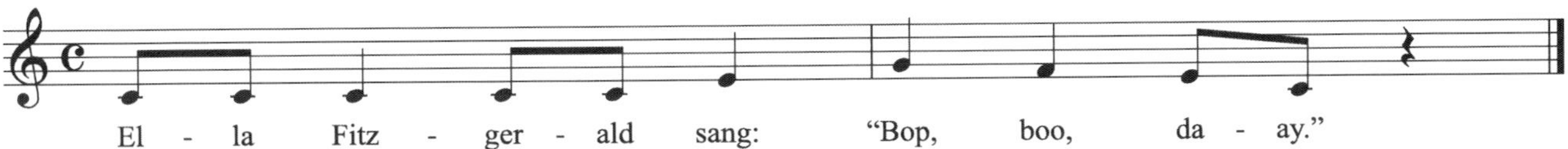

Adding Some Rhythm

It is also fun to improvise using rhythm. We like to create rhythmic patterns by tapping or patting our bodies. For example, clap your hands and pat your head. Begin by having the students repeat the pattern. Once the children get the hang of it, they will have fun creating their own rhythmic patterns. Rhythmic patterns are made up of long and short sounds. For example:

Teacher: clap, clap, head, head (long, long, long, long)

Class: clap, clap, head, head

Teacher: clap, clap, head, head, head (long, long, short, short, short)

Class: clap, clap, head, head, head

Teacher: knees, clap, clap, knees (long, long, long, long)

Class: knees, clap, clap, knees

Teacher: knees, clap, clap, knees, clap (long, short, short, long, long)

Class: knees, clap, clap, knees, clap

Teacher: tummy, tummy, chest, chest (short, short, short, short, long, long)

Class: tummy, tummy, chest, chest

Teacher: tummy, chest, tummy, chest (short, short, long, short, short, long)

Class: tummy, chest, tummy, chest

Ella Rhythm Chant

Lousie Rogers

Change the Ella chant so that the class is chanting "Ella Fitzgerald – she had rhythm." Have the class sit in a circle. Work your way around the circle asking each child to create another pattern. In between each improvisation, the class chants or sings the chant above.

Extensions

Drums

Playing the drums will enhance this poem and is a lot of fun! There are several ways to incorporate the drums, depending on ability and resources.

- To simulate a swing feel, the teacher can play on beats 2 and 4.

  Depending on age and ability, your students may be able to:

- Play the swing feel as an accompaniment.

- Solo on their drums in the same way that they performed rhythm solos on their bodies. Between solos, the class can chant "Ella Fitzgerald – she had rhythm."

  If you have access to instruments such as xylophones and glockenspiels, then you may also consider adding an instrumental solo section:

- Change the chant to "Ella Fitzgerald, she had a band."

- Set up the instruments in C Major pentatonic to keep the tonality.

Note to Teachers: C Major pentatonic contains the notes CDEGA. (Take off all of the bars on the instruments except for the notes CDEGA.) On a keyboard or piano, it is helpful to use sticky labels or colored pieces of tape on which the note names are written.

Bebop — Charlie Parker

*"Music is your own experience, your own thoughts, your wisdom.
If you don't live it, it won't come out your horn."*
attributed to Charlie Parker

JAZZ GREAT—Charles "Yardbird" Parker (1920–1955)

Charles Parker was an amazing saxophonist who gained wide recognition for his brilliant solos and innovative improvisations. He was, without a doubt, one of the most influential and talented musicians in jazz history.

Charlie Parker was born on August 29, 1920 in Kansas City, Kansas. When he was a young child, his family moved to Kansas City, Missouri. He loved music and when he was 15, he started playing the alto saxophone. He played in the school band. Soon, he was playing in local jazz and blues bands.

Charlie joined several bands and eventually moved to New York City. He met and played with other jazz greats such as Miles Davis, Dizzy Gillespie and Thelonius Monk. He played a leading role in the development of Bebop, the jazz style characterized by fast tempos and improvisation. He composed many songs and he traveled all around the world playing his music.

Charlie Parker's nickname was the BIRD or YARDBIRD. The famous jazz nightclub BIRDLAND in New York City was named in his honor. There are many stories about how he got that nickname. Some say it's because his favorite food was chicken!

Charlie Parker Teaching Suggestions

Tell the class a little bit about Charlie Parker. Be sure to mention:

- Charlie Parker was born in Kansas City, Kansas and moved to Kansas City, Missouri when he was a young child.

- Charlie loved music and started playing the alto saxophone when he was 15 years old.

- Charlie played in his high school band and local jazz and blues bands.

- Charlie moved to New York City and played with jazz greats such as Miles Davis, Dizzy Gillespie and Thelonius Monk.

- Charlie's nickname was Bird or Yardbird. The jazz club Birdland was named in his honor.

Bebop

Charlie Parker is credited with being one of the developers of Bebop music in the 1940s. Bebop was played in small groups rather than in big bands. The musicians had the opportunity to solo, which allowed them to show off their musical talents. Bebop was not as popular with the general public as swing music and was never the pop music of its day.

Charlie Parker Played Bebop

Materials Needed

- The book, *Charlie Parker Played Bebop* by Chris Raschka

- Track # on CD

Procedure

- Read the book to the children before playing the recording on the CD. This is helpful because the recording moves along quickly. The children will benefit from hearing the words and having time to look at the illustrations prior to singing along with the CD.

- Point out some of the interesting illustrations of Charlie Parker, the saxophone, birds and bird feet, etc. You may want to talk about the phrase "Never leave your cat alone." This phrase has prompted many discussions. What does it mean? Does it have something to do with birds and cats? We don't know what the answer is, but we certainly enjoy hearing all of the ideas that the children have.

- Finally, play the CD while showing the pictures in the book.

- Play the CD twice, allowing the children to listen the first time, and sing along the second time. (On the recording, each page is sung twice, giving the children a second chance to hear it and sing it.)

- Read the book to the class, allowing the children to echo each page. Vary your pitch, tempo and volume. Whisper and shout. Make your voice high in pitch and low in pitch. Say some lines slowly and some quickly. Repeat as many lines as you like.

Have the book and CD available in your listening area for children to enjoy on their own.

Improvising with Charlie Parker Played Be Bop

Improvisation is spontaneously composing, rhythmically and/or melodically, within the structure of the music. When we improvise with our voices, we sing with made-up words and sounds. We call this "scatting."

Scat: "Scat" is a jazz language used by vocalists when trying to make their voices sound like instruments. The singer sings made-up words and a made-up melody that "fit" or sound good over the chords of the piece. When you are scatting, you are playing with sounds, which is an age appropriate literacy and music activity for young children and a whole lot of fun. For more information about scatting, see Chapter 1.

- Whether you are singing or speaking your scat phrases, we encourage you to explore your voice and have fun! Adding some of the following musical elements will help to make your scat phrases more interesting and diverse:

- Dynamics—the loudness or softness of your voice.

- Crescendos—allowing your voice to slowly get louder.

- Decrescendos—allowing your voice to slowly get softer.

- Slides—sliding your voice from one note to another.

- Rests—allowing pauses in your scat phrases.

- Inflection—changing the tone or pitch of your voice while either speaking or singing. This happens naturally as we speak. We do not speak in a monotone. For example, when we ask a question, our voice usually goes up in pitch at the end of the sentence.

- High voice and low voice—changing out of your natural register. How high can you go? How low can you go? Experiment.

- Rhythmic Diversity—long words and short words.

- Patterns—creating rhythmic and/or melodic patterns.

- Syncopation—a syncopated rhythm is one that delivers an element of rhythmic surprise.

Materials Needed

- *Charlie Parker Played Bebop* riff (see below)

- Instruments of your choice (see instrumental set-up below)

Procedure

- Explain to the children that they will each have a turn to improvise. The class may improvise by using their voices, by clapping, by tapping a rhythm on a drum, a desk, a chair, the floor, the body, etc., or by playing an instrument. See below for suggestions on how to set up and choose the instruments.

- If you are using the voice alone, this is a great opportunity to discuss playing with words in the way that Chris Raschka does in his book. Unlike Ella Fitzgerald, Chris Raschka does not use scat syllables (buh–buh-duh) to improvise. Mr. Raschka uses words, sounds and onomatopoeias in a playful and rhythmic way, incorporating elements of jazz such as syncopation, rhythmic diversity, and improvisation. For more on Ella Fitzgerald and her style of scatting, see chapter one.

- Have the class sit in a circle. Teach the class the *Charlie Parker Played Bebop* riff. This can either be spoken or sung. The riff is the exact same melody and rhythm that is heard at the beginning of the recording. If you are not comfortable singing, feel free to just speak it in rhythm.

- Sing/speak the riff and then the first child in the circle has an opportunity to improvise a solo.

- After every solo, sing the riff again. The solo should last two measures. However, if the soloist is having fun and being creative, let him or her have more time.

- When the soloist is finished, cue the class to sing/speak the riff again. Repeat until everyone has had a turn to improvise.

Charlie Parker Played Bebop Riff

Instrumental Set-Up

- Set up the instruments in the key of F Pentatonic (F, G, A, C, D).

- Instrument suggestions: glockenspiel, resonator bars, bells, piano, xylophone, etc. (Take off all of the E and B bars. For the piano, identify the available notes (F, G, A, C, & D) with stickers or tape,)

  Percussion Instruments: drums, rhythm sticks, wood blocks, slit drums, shakers, etc. (It is fun to use just one shaker so that it is possible to clap with the shaker. With one hand free and one hand holding the shaker, there are a lot of possibilities and it's easier to be more rhythmic.)

Adding Instrumental Accompaniment

The accompaniment below can be added. It can be played by the teacher, a student, or a group of students. The improvised solos occur exactly as described in the "Improvising with Charlie Parker Played Bebop section in this chapter.

Charlie Parker Riff Accompaniment

Extensions

A Night in Tunisia

- Materials needed :

- A recording of the song "A Night in Tunisia" played by Charlie Parker

  The book *Charlie Parker Played Bebop* by Chris Raschka

Procedure

- Play "A Night in Tunisia" and explain how Chris Raschka was inspired by this piece to write the book, *Charlie Parker Played Bebop*.

- Now, read the book to the class, allowing children to echo each page. Vary your pitch, tempo and volume. Whisper and shout. Use vocal inflection to explore some high notes and low notes. Say some lines slowly and some quickly. Repeat as many lines as you like.

- Play the music again and see if the kids can identify any of the musical phrases with the language in the book. For example, the phrase, "Never leave your cat alone," or the phrase, "Charlie Parker played Bebop."

- Read the book again. Encourage the children to interpret and improvise.

Chapter 3

Cool Jazz — Miles Davis

"My future starts when I wake up every morning.
Every day I find something creative to do with my life."
attributed to Miles Davis

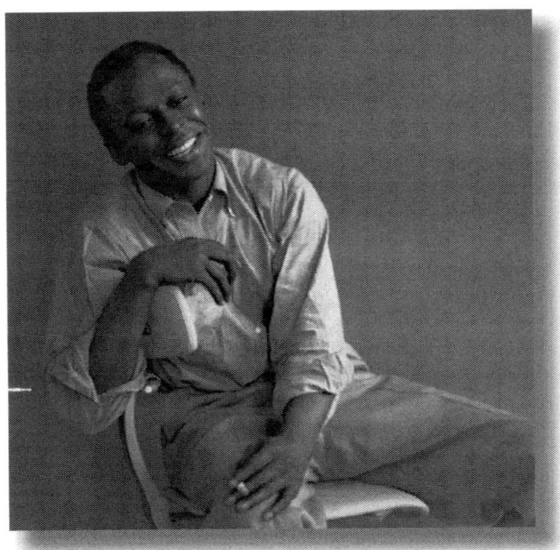

JAZZ GREAT—Miles Davis (1926–1991)

Miles Davis played the trumpet. He was born on May 26, 1926 and grew up in East St. Louis, Illinois where his father was a well-to-do dentist. At the age of 13, Miles' father bought him a trumpet and arranged for him to take lessons from one of his patients. This teacher, Elwood Buchanan, was a big influence on Miles and helped shape the sound that Miles Davis is so well known for, a beautiful, rich and melodic tone with very little vibrato.

In 1945, Miles moved to New York City and attended the Juilliard School of Music. After just a short time at Juilliard, Miles decided to leave the school and try his hand at performing and composing in the world of jazz.

Miles was influenced and inspired by the great saxophonist, Charlie Parker, also known as the "Bird." When he first came to the city, Miles hoped to find Parker. He searched for him but Parker was not so easy to find in the big city of New York! Davis longed to meet him and play with him. Legend has it that Charlie knew Miles was looking for him. The story goes that one night, at a jam session at a club in Harlem called **The Heatwave**, as Miles stepped outside to get some fresh air, he heard a voice say, "Hello, Miles ... I hear you've been looking for me." It was Charlie Parker. Parker invited Miles to play with him. This eventually led to Davis' recording debut, playing with Charlie Parker.

Miles Davis proved himself to be a creative force in the world of jazz. His musical explorations helped lead the way to the development of many new styles of jazz, including Bebop and Cool Jazz. (For more on Bebop and Cool Jazz, see the Appendix.) Davis wrote many compositions and was a highly respected band leader. Above all, though, Miles was known for his distinctive sound on the trumpet. He often played with a mute and his sound was rich, mellow, beautiful, melodic, rhythmic, and exciting.

Miles Davis Teaching Suggestions

- Tell the class a little bit about Miles Davis. Be sure to mention:

- Miles Davis started playing the trumpet at age 13.

- His trumpet teacher Elwood Buchanan helped Miles develop his beautiful rich melodic tone.

- He grew up in Illinois, but moved to New York City to attend Julliard School of Music and to search for his idol, Charlie Parker whom he eventually met and played with.

- Miles was a creative force in the jazz world and helped develop Bebop and cool jazz. He was also a composer. "So What" is one of his most well-known compositions.

Cool Jazz

Developed in the late 1940s, Cool Jazz was influenced by modern classical music. It was more relaxed than swing, and easier to follow than Bebop.

Teaching Suggestions

Note to Teachers: The repetitive nature of this piece makes it easy to learn. First listen to the piece before teaching it to the class. As you listen, pay close attention to the phrase "so what," as you will be teaching it to the class and it will be important to model the correct inflecion.

So What

- Explain to the class that you will be reading a poem about Miles Davis and that they will need to help out by saying the phrase "So what."

- Model the tone for the kids so that no one is yelling the phrase.

- The phrase has a natural inflection with the emphasis on the word "so."

- We like to say the phrase with a slight crescendo. The word "so" gets just a little bit louder (crescendo).

- You can also point out that the phrase consists of a long note/word ("so") and a short note/word ("what"). Modeling the tone will help to make this short phrase more musical. Rhythmically, "so" is held for a dotted quarter note and "what" is notated by an eighth note. (See written music above.)

- Have the class repeat after you as you emphasize this pattern "Long-short," "Long-short," "Long-short." As you say this, add the crescendos.

- Now, change it to "So what!," "So what!," "So what!"

- Now, read the poem/lyrics to the class and have them interject the words "So what!" at the appropriate places.

- Explain to the class that Charlie Parker was a great musician who played the saxophone and was greatly admired by Miles Davis. For more information about Charlie Parker, see Chapter 3.

The Lyrics

So What

Music by Miles Davis, lyrics by Louise Rogers

Materials needed

Verse 1
Said Miles Davis was his name.
So what!
And playing trumpet was his game.
So what!
Said Miles Davis was his name.
So what!
He played the game.
So what!

Verse 2
He played all day and every night.
So what!
Those trumpet lines were out of sight.
So what!
He played all day and every night.
So what!
He's out of sight.
So what!

Verse 3
Now, Charlie Parker, he's the "Bird."
So what!
The "Bird" said Davis is the word.
So what!
Now, Charlie Parker, he's the "Bird."
So what!
Davis is the word.
So what!

Verse 4
Said Miles Davis was his name.
So what!
And playing trumpet was his game.
So what!
Said Miles Davis was his name.
So what!
He played the game.
So what!

(these last 2 lines can repeat and fade out—getting softer each time)

Procedure

Engage the class in a discussion about the lyrics to the song. Consider the following phrases:

- "So what"

  "So what" is a phrase said in such a way as to try to make others think that you don't care about something that you really do care about.

- "And playing trumpet was his game."

  Miles Davis played the trumpet for a living and for enjoyment. It is what he did! What's your game?

- "Those trumpet lines were out of sight."

  "Lines" refers to musical phrases. "Out of sight" means that it was amazing! Can you think of something that you think is "out of sight?"

- "Charlie Parker, he's the Bird."

  Charlie Parker's nickname was "the Bird." Do you or does anyone you know have a nickname?

- "The "Bird" said Davis is the word."

  "The word" means something is very important and generally the best that there is. Charlie Parker was very highly regarded, so for him to say that Davis was "the word" really meant a lot. Can you think of someone else who is "the word?"

The Recording

Play the recording (Track # ?) for the class. Explain to them that on the recording they will hear Louise and some children singing the song "So What." The words to the song were written by Louise and they tell us about Miles Davis. It's important to remind everyone that Miles Davis composed the music and originally it was played just by the trumpet with no singing and no words.

Point out to them that there is a vocal solo that the singer (Louise) learned by listening to Miles Davis' solo on the instrumental version. She copied exactly what Miles played on his trumpet and then sang it. We call this transcribing.

Singing Along

Below are the notes to the words "So what!" that are sung by the children on the recording.

Note to Teachers: The first measure contains the "So what!" notes (notes B-A) for the first, second and fourth verses. There is a key change at the third verse. The second measure contains the "So what!" notes (notes C-B♭) for the third verse. The fourth verse, changes back to the original key and back to the first measure notes. The key change may sound difficult, but you will be surprised how easily the kids will do this!

So What

Extensions

- Play a recording of Miles Davis playing "So What." For suggested recordings, see the Appendix.

- Have a discussion about the phrase "So what." Ask the children if they have ever said the phrase when they were pretending that they didn't care about something, but actually they really did care a lot.

- Have the class write their own lyrics to the song.

  This could be done as a class, in small groups, with a partner, or by one person.

  The lyrics do not need to be about Miles Davis.

  Some examples:

  And now it's time to clean my room

  So what!

  I'll sweep the floor and get the broom

  So what!

  OR

  Now jazz is fun to sing and play

  So what!

  We scat and sing a Bop Boo Day

  So What!

- Read the book *Looking for Bird in the Big City* by Robert Burleigh and Marek Los.

- Discuss how excited Miles was to meet Bird.

- Why do you think he was so excited to meet Bird?

- Have you ever been that excited to meet someone? Why?

- Is there anyone special who you would like to meet? Why? Where could you find this person? Where could you look?

- Act out the book.

- Invite the children to tell you stories about looking for someone or something special. Act out the children's stories.

Dixieland — Louis Armstrong

"Nobody played it like they played it in New Orleans, a city already used to feeling jubilant, and expressing its jubilation. A city where you could dance down the middle of the street, in the middle of the daytime, in the middle of the week, and instead of people wondering why you weren't at work, they'd be wondering how they could join you. The glory of New Orleans is that it's still that way today. Everyone loves a parade. Everything is touched by the joyous anarchy called New Orleans Jazz. And everybody's middle name is 'Celebrate.'"
The New Orleans Tourism Marketing Corporation, 1996

JAZZ GREAT — *Louis "Satchmo" Armstrong (1901–1971)*

Louis "Satchmo" Armstrong was born on August 4, 1901 in New Orleans, "the birthplace of jazz." His family was very poor and he left school after the third grade to go to work delivering coal. He loved music and taught himself to play the cornet. As he grew older, he played in the marching and jazz bands that were becoming very popular in the city. He also played on Mississippi riverboats. He is strongly identified with the Dixieland music of the era. He joined King Oliver's Creole Jazz Band in 1922 and moved to Chicago. In 1924, he moved to New York City to join the Fletcher Henderson Orchestra. He moved back to Chicago in 1925 and played in various bands there until 1929, when he returned to New York. After that, he began to play all over the United States, Canada and Europe.

Legend has it that he became the world's very first scat singer when he dropped his lyrics to "Heebie Jeebies" on the floor in a recording session and continued singing, using nonsense syllables and making his voice sound like an instrument.

Louis had a long career playing trumpet, singing, and even acting and dancing in Broadway shows and movies! He influenced many other instrumentalists and singers. Because of his wide smile and big cheeks, people gave him the nickname "Satchel Mouth" later shortened to "Satchmo." His unique sounding voice and infectious bubbly personality endeared him to people throughout the world!

Louis Armstrong Teaching Suggestions

Tell the class a little bit about Louis Armstrong. Be sure to mention:

- Louis Armstrong was born in New Orleans, Louisiana, "the birthplace of jazz."

- Louis was very poor and had to leave school after the third grade to go to work. He taught himself how to play the cornet.

- Louis played in jazz and marching bands in New Orleans.

- Legend has it that he was the world's very first scat singer when he dropped his lyrics and had to improvise.

- People gave Louis the nickname Satchelmouth or "Satchmo" because of his wide smile and big cheeks.

Dixieland

Dixieland is a style of jazz music. A Dixieland band is made up of a rhythm section consisting of drums, piano, tuba or bass, and banjo or guitar. The front line or lead instruments include trumpet or cornet, clarinet and trombone.

Dixieland started in New Orleans at the beginning of the last century and then spread to New York and Chicago. It is the earliest recorded style of jazz music combining brass band marches, ragtime and blues.

When you hear Dixieland music, it makes you want to march. It is very popular with young children who love the strong rhythms, upbeat tempos, and joyous sounds.

Parades

Everyone loves a parade, especially young children! In our experience, parades always get an enthusiastic response and serve multiple functions in the early childhood classroom.

Parades can aid in classroom management. If children are feeling antsy and are becoming unfocused, a parade refocuses and reorganizes them. And, if you are transitioning children to the playground, gym, or art room, a parade can help to get them there in a positive, joyful way. Parades also teach children how to follow directions and how to function as a group. Most importantly, in terms of our work, parades introduce musical concepts in an age-appropriate and very enjoyable way.

As educators of young children know, children learn best through their play. As they "play" marching in a real parade, they learn musical, social and academic skills. They can improvise movements, keep the beat, cooperate with others, and play real and imaginary instruments as they pretend to be marching in a real parade. There is no more effective way to learn.

Educational Concepts

1.) How to keep a beat—the understanding of how to keep a beat is the primary musical concept practiced by participating in a parade. Children can "find the beat" and move their bodies or march in time to music. They can add percussion instruments, such as shakers or drums. Singing can be added, as well. To do all three together requires a sophisticated coordination of effort and can take some practice. For some children, just walking in a line will be an accomplishment, but, with practice, they will begin to feel the beat in their bodies through the strong rhythm of the parade music.

2.) Identifying musical instruments—children will also learn how to listen for and distinguish musical instruments and hear how they combine and blend together as a band. By adding their own percussion instrument to the mix the children are, in effect, playing with the band.

3.) Identifying the melody—by learning the song and singing along, children will learn how to identify the melody line in a piece of music.

Let's Imagine a Parade

Explore the concept of a parade using the picture book *Parade* by Donald Crews and the Dixieland jazz music of Louis Armstrong.

Materials needed

- A recording of "When the Saints go Marching In" by Louis Armstrong

- *Parade* by Donald Crews

Procedure

- First read the book to the class. The book describes the course of a parade from early morning when signs are put up announcing that there will be a parade that day. It goes on to show the crowds gathering to watch the parade, listening for the first sounds of the parade in the distance, the parade passing by in all its glory, and even the clean-up after the parade is over.

- After reading the book, ask the children about parades that they might have seen either in person or on television.

- Then read the book again but this time add the Dixieland music "When the Saints Go Marching In" to bring the parade to life. Start out with the volume low as the parade approaches the awaiting crowd and increase the volume as the participants in the parade pass by. Then reduce the volume again as the parade marches off into the distance.

Extension

Play "When the Saints Go Marching In" again. Discuss the Dixieland music you hear with the children.

- Dynamics—When is the music loud? When is it soft?

- Rhythm—How many ways can you move your body to the beat? Does the beat make you want to march in the parade?

- Instruments—What instruments did you hear?

Let's Have a Parade

Materials needed

- A recording of "When the Saints Go Marching In" by Louis Armstrong

- Shakers

    Songs by other artists that are great for marching:

- Dixieland Stars: "Bill Bailey"

- Sam Levine: "Battle Hymn of the Republic"

- Green Hill Instrumental: "Alexander's Ragtime Band"

Procedure: Practice feeling the beat

- Play the recording of "When the Saints Go Marching In" and listen to it for a while.

- Help the children find the beat with their bodies. First move just your head to the beat, then add the shoulders, elbows, hips, knees, etc.

- Clap the beat with your hands. Use your hands to tap the beat on your heads, chests, tummies, and knees.

- Finally feel the beat in your feet by marching in place. Practice until the children are comfortable with the beat. Now you are ready for the parade to begin.

Before the Parade Begins

Explain to the children that you are going to recreate the parade in your classroom. Discuss the ground rules:

- They will follow one another in a line behind a designated leader.

- They will keep the beat with the movement of their feet.

- They will be careful to avoid crashing into anyone or anything.

- Plan the parade route you will take around the classroom or consider going outside of the classroom.

- Shakers can be added to keep the beat with a sound.

The Parade

- Line up the children and designate a leader. Initially it should be a teacher, but after several repetitions, a child might be able to take a turn as a leader.

- Invite the children to use their imaginations as they pretend to march down the street and play instruments, wave at spectators, wear costumes, etc.

- Then put on the music and have a great time at your classroom Mardi Gras! (For more about Mardi Gras, see the Appendix.)

Variation: Rhythm Stick Band

Materials needed

- Rhythm sticks

- Recorded music by Louis Armstrong such as "When the Saints go Marching In," "Bourbon Street Parade," "Bill Bailey"

Procedure

- Play the recorded music and listen to it for a while. Listen for the singing voices. Try to identify the instruments you hear.

- Help the children find the beat by clapping their hands.

- Show the children the rhythm sticks and demonstrate how you tap them together to keep a rhythm. Explain how to use them properly and safely and how they must never wave them around or touch anyone else with them. Emphasize that rhythm sticks are musical instruments and should be treated as such.

- Hand out two rhythm sticks to each child and give the children ample time to practice using them. Practice keeping a steady beat with the rhythm sticks.

- Play the recorded music again, keeping the beat first by clapping hands, and then using the rhythm sticks to keep the beat.

- Experiment with improvising rhythmic patterns that fit with the music.

- Give the children a cue to start improvising, and then a cue to return to the steady beat. Practice alternating improvisation with steady beats. You can also divide the class into two groups and let one group keep the steady beat while the other improvises.

Extensions

- Add rhythm sticks to the parade to make a rhythm stick marching band.

- Make rhythm instruments of your own. For example, fill empty water bottles with sand, rice, or beans to make shakers. For other shaker ideas, see Chapter 7.

- Create costumes such as colorful hats adorned with feathers and glitter to wear at your parade.

- Improvise movements as you march. For example, sway from side to side, march backwards, or add a turn.

- Try some of the other pieces of parade music listed in the Appendix.

- Read other parade books such as *Thump Thump Rat a Tat Tat* by Gene Baer and Lois Ehlert.

- Read other books about dixieland jazz and New Orleans such as *The Jazz of our Street* by Fatima Shaik.

- Listen to some more Louis Armstrong songs and read more about his life in *When Louis Armstrong Taught Me Scat* by Muriel Harris Weinstein, and *Horn for Louis* by Eric Kimmel.

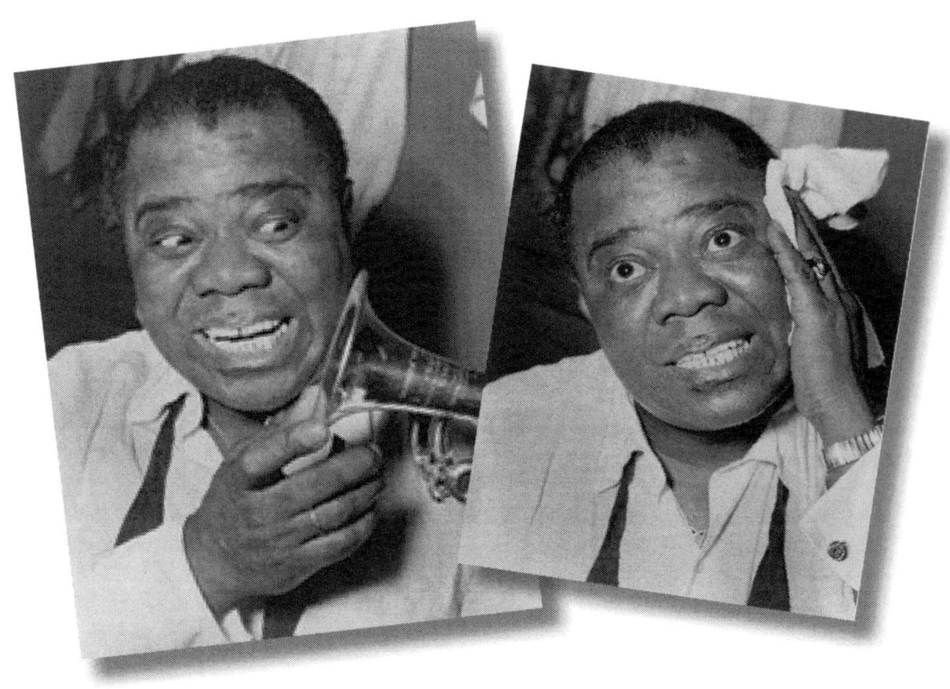

Chapter 5

Swing and Big Band — Duke Ellington

*"The most important thing I look for in a musician
is whether he knows how to listen."* Duke Ellington

JAZZ GREAT — *Edward Kennedy "Duke" Ellington (1899–1974)*

Duke Ellington was born on April 29, 1899 in Washington, D.C. He started taking piano lessons when he was seven years old and began his professional career when he was still a teenager. It is said that he got his nickname from one of his friends because of his elegant manners and dress.

When he was in his twenties, he moved to New York City and played at the Cotton Club, the most famous jazz nightclub in Harlem. The Duke is strongly identified with the swing jazz music of the big band era and was the leader of the Duke Ellington Orchestra. He composed thousands of songs! He called his music "American Music" and influenced many other jazz musicians. "Take the A Train" was composed by his collaborator, the pianist and composer Billy Strayhorn, and became the signature piece of the Duke Ellington Orchestra.

Duke Ellington had a 50 year career and played over 20,000 performances all over the world. He even acted in several movies. He received many awards in his life, including the Grammy Lifetime Achievement award in 1966; the Presidential Medal of Freedom from Richard Nixon in 1969; and the French Legion of Honor in 1973.

When Duke Ellington died, more than 12,000 people attended his funeral. Ella Fitzgerald was said to have observed, "It's a very sad day. A genius has passed." For more on Ella Fitzgerald, see Chapter 1.

Duke Ellington Teaching Suggestions

Tell the class a little bit about Duke Ellington. Be sure to mention:

- Duke Ellington started taking piano lessons when he was only seven years old, and began his professional career when he was still a teenager.

- Duke played big band swing jazz music and was the leader of his own orchestra, who's signature song was "Take the A Train."

- Duke's real name was Edward Kennedy Ellington, but he got the nickname "Duke" because of his elegant manners and dress.

- Duke composed thousands of songs and called his music "American Music."

Tell the class a little about swing music.

Swing and the Big Band Era

Swing music was extremely popular and, simply put, made a person want to dance and move. The swing bands were large. A typical "Big Band" or "Jazz Orchestra" might have 12–25 members: trombones, trumpets, saxophones, woodwinds, piano, drums, bass, guitar, vibraphone, etc. These "Big Bands" and "Jazz Orchestras" performed at dance halls such as the Savoy Ballroom in New York City and at concert halls such as Carnegie Hall. Swing music became the popular music of the day.

Take the A Train

Tell the class a little about subways.

- London opened the first subway in the world in 1863.

- There are about 160 subway systems in the world.

- New York City has the most stations and the longest amount of track.

- *Subway Ride* by Heather Lynne Miller will introduce them to subways all over the world.

Tell the class a little about the "A" Train.

- The "A" train is a world famous subway train in New York City.

- It runs from Brooklyn through Harlem, to northern Manhattan.

- Introduce them to this world-famous subway train by reading a picture book about it, such as *Subway* by Christoph Niemann; *My Subway Ride* by Paul DuBois Jacobs; or *Subway* by Anastasia Suen.

- Discuss the repetitive rhythm of the "A" train. Children who have ridden on trains, even child-sized ones at zoos and amusement parks, will know exactly what you mean. There is a rhythmic pattern associated with trains as they move along the tracks. The "A" train has a kidonk-a-donk, kidonk-a-donk rhythm.

Billy Strayhorn

Billy Strayhorn was a young man in his early twenties when he composed "Take the A Train." Billy was an accomplished pianist and came to New York to join the Duke Ellington Orchestra. He loved to compose his own music. It is possible that he might have been inspired by the rhythmic beat of the "A" train as he rode it for the first time in 1939. However, some tell the story that Billy was inspired by handwritten directions to the Apollo Theater that Duke sent him: "Be sure to take the "A" train if you want to go to Harlem." The "A" train had only been in service for three years at the time.

For more on the Apollo Theater, see the Appendix.

Young children rarely have knowledge about how songs came to be. Sometimes children think that music comes from iPods, CDs, or radios. Some think that songs have always been in the world, like grass or trees. It is important that children understand that music is composed by real people who are often inspired by things going on around them, and that children can also compose music of their own.

Tell the class a little about Billy Strayhorn. Be sure to mention:

- Billy Strayhorn was a pianist and composer who collaborated with Duke Ellington.

- He composed "Take the A Train" when he was in his early twenties.

- He may have been inspired by the rhythm of the "A" train as he rode it for the first time.

- He may have been inspired by a note Duke sent him with directions to the Apollo Theater—"Be sure to take the "A" train if you want to go to Harlem."

Teaching Suggestions
Let's Ride on the "A" Train

Materials needed: a recording of "Take the A Train" For recording suggestions, please see the Appendix.

- Play "Take the A Train" for the children. Have them remain seated and ask them to use their imaginations to pretend that they are riding on the train. Tell them to bounce up and down in time to the music.

- Now, ask them to stand up so they can feel the rhythm in various parts of their bodies. First tell them to move their heads in time to the music. Then isolate other parts of the body in a similar manner— shoulders, knees, feet, arms, fingers, and so on, giving ample opportunity for everyone to master the rhythm.

- Now pretend that you are all on the train. Some children can sit while others can stand, pretending to hold on to poles. At each stop, "ding dong," the doors open. You can open your arms to represent the doors opening. Imagine passengers getting off and new ones entering the train. Then "ding dong," the doors close. You can close your arms to represent the doors closing. Then the train moves on.

Extension

While the music is playing, talk about the subway stops they are passing on their way uptown—42nd Street., 59th Street, etc. The Apollo Theater is on 125th Street. For a list of "A" Train stops, please see the Appendix.

Variation: Add instruments of your own. For example:

- Bells or bars for the doors opening

- Sticks, blocks or shakers for going along the tracks

- Drums for the brakes

Let's Be the "A" Train

Materials needed: a recording of "Take the A Train." For recommendations, please see the Appendix.

Note to teachers: You will be making a parade with the children, so it is important to discuss the guidelines carefully with them before you begin. Below are a few suggestions:

- The children will follow one another in a single line behind a designated leader.

- They will be careful to move at the same speed as the person in front of them to avoid crashing into anyone or anything.

- They will follow a route designated by you that you will take around the classroom, or out of the classroom.

- They will keep the beat with the movement of their feet.

- Shakers can be added to keep the beat with a sound.

Procedure

- Ask the children to imagine that they are the cars of the "A" train itself. They will be making a kind of parade, a parade of subway cars.

- Give each child a shaker. Practice by marching in place, shaking the shakers before the "train" moves on down the track.

- Now line up the children and designate a leader. It should be a teacher the first time, but after several repetitions, a child might be able to take a turn as the leader.

- Play "Take the A Train." As you follow your designated route around the room, make some stops along the way. This will give the children additional practice in taking directions, starting and stopping their playing and marching, and participating in music together as a group.

Lyrics

Lyrics are words written to music. Many people have been inspired to write lyrics to "Take the A Train." One of them was a young woman named Joya Sherrill who, in 1944, was listening to her radio at her home in Chicago and heard the Duke Ellington Orchestra playing "Take the A Train." It so inspired her that she wrote lyrics to the song as she listened to it. Duke Ellington liked the words to the song so much that he hired her to sing the lyrics with his orchestra.

Ella Fitzgerald sang and recorded the song many times adding her own inventive scat singing to the lyrics. Over the years many singers and musicians have played and sung the song. It became one of the most famous songs of the twentieth century.

Teaching Suggestions

Compare instrumental and lyricized versions.

- First, listen to an instrumental version of "Take the A Train."

- Next, listen to Ella Fitzgerald singing the lyrics and scatting.

- Compare the two. Do you prefer one over the other? How do words change the way you understand the meaning of the song?

Teach the class the lyrics (this is one version of many)

You must take the A Train

To go to Sugar Hill way up in Harlem

If you miss the A Train

You'll find you've missed the quickest way to Harlem

Hurry, get on, now, it's coming

Listen to those rails a-thrumming (All Aboard!)

Get on the A Train

Soon you will be on Sugar Hill in Harlem

Collaboration

Duke Ellington collaborated with Billy Strayhorn and many musicians in his orchestra. Collaboration means teamwork, and jazz is all about teamwork. Creative ideas ignite other creative ideas. When individuals contribute ideas, listen to each other, and work together, amazing results can happen. Sharing ideas is a great way to work.

Teaching Suggestion

Jazzy Train Collaborative Art Project

Materials needed:

- Rectangular pieces of cardboard or foam core
- Assorted collage materials
- Roll of paper
- Paste
- Crayons or markers

Procedure

- Set up the materials at tables with one piece of cardboard or foam core for two children.
- Explain that by working in pairs, they will create a car for a jazzy train, using collage materials. After the cars are completed we will put them all together to make the train.
- Play a recording of "Take the A Train" for inspiration while they are working.
- Explain that each pair will need to discuss what they want to do with each other before they begin. They can divide the project in half if they wish, or both work on the whole thing together.
- After the cars are finished, assemble them on a roll of paper on which the children can draw a track. Then display the train on a wall or bulletin board.

Variations

- Make an alphabet train using 26 cars each labeled with a letter of the alphabet—
an ABCDEFGHIJKLMNOPQRSTUVWXYZ train.
- Make a number train labeling each car with a different number. In New York City, for example, some trains have numbers like the 1, 2 and 9 trains, instead of letters.
- Add photographs of the children to the train cars.

Extensions

- Read more books about subways and trains. See the Appendix.
- Read more about Duke Ellington. See the Appendix.
- Listen to some of Duke Ellington's 3000 songs. See the Appendix.
- Dance to some of his big band swing music.
- Look at a New York City subway map, and trace the entire route of the A train.
You can find one at www.mta.info/maps/

Chapter 6

Swing — Benny Goodman

*"It takes the black keys and the white keys both,
to make perfect harmony."*
Benny Goodman's reply when he was asked as to
why he had an integrated band.

JAZZ GREAT—*Benny Goodman (1909–1986)*

Benny Goodman was born on May 30, 1909, and grew up in Chicago, Illinois. He had eleven brothers and sisters. He started playing the clarinet at age 10. By the time he was only 14, he was playing professionally. At age 16, he moved to California to join Ben Pollock's band. After getting all of this experience under his belt, Benny decided to move to New York City to try to make it on his own.

In New York City, Benny played with many musicians and was very successful. He was an important figure in the development of the Big Band era. 1934 was an important year for him when Benny Goodman's first big band auditioned for the new Billy Rose Music Hall Theater Restaurant. Benny and the band got the job!

Radio shows were popular in those days and Benny Goodman's Big Band was chosen to be on an innovative show based in California called *Let's Dance*. His band really swung and people loved to dance to his music!

Benny Goodman also enjoyed playing in smaller groups. With his new drummer, Gene Krupa, Teddy Wilson on piano, and Lionel Hampton on the xylophone, their quartet became one of the first integrated jazz groups in the United States. The Benny Goodman Quartet played the famous Paramount Theater, and Carnegie Hall in New York City. Benny Goodman was known as the "King of Swing."

Benny Goodman Teaching Suggestions

Tell the class a little bit about Benny Goodman. Be sure to mention:

- Benny Goodman started playing the clarinet at age 10, and by age 16 moved to California to play in a professional band.

- He was an important person in the development of the Big Band era, and was known as the "King of Swing."

- Benny Goodman's big band played on the radio show *Let's Dance*. People loved to dance to his swing music.

- Benny, Gene Krupa, Teddy Wilson, and Lionel Hampton formed a quartet which was one of the first integrated jazz groups in the United States.

Swing and the Big Band Era

Swing music was extremely popular between 1935 and 1945 with the development of big bands and jazz orchestras. Simply put, swing music made a person want to dance and move. A typical "Big Band" or "Jazz Orchestra" might have 12–25 members, and included many instruments such as: trombones, trumpets, saxophones, woodwinds, piano, drums, bass, guitar, and vibraphone. These "Big Bands" and "Jazz Orchestras" performed at dance halls such as the Savoy Ballroom in New York City, and at concert halls such as Carnegie Hall. The music became the popular music of the day. During this swing era, other popular big bands were led by Glenn Miller, Duke Ellington, Chick Webb, Artie Shaw, and Count Basie, among others.

Movement and Dance to Recorded Music

One of the simplest and most effective ways to add musical experiences to the school day is to play recorded music and allow children the opportunity to respond to the music through movement or dance. It is a wonderful way to begin the day, transition from one subject area to another, or introduce an art or music lesson. Benny Goodman recorded an enormous number of dance tunes which young children respond to in a positive and enthusiastic way.

Free Dance

Materials needed: Recorded music. Here are a few Benny Goodman songs that are great for dancing.

- "Sing Sing Sing"

- "Stompin' at the Savoy"

- "King Porter Stomp"

Procedure

- Put on recorded music and listen to it for awhile.

- Encourage the children to move to the rhythms they hear while seated

- Encourage the children to stand up and move around to the music.

- If all of the adults in the room dance with the children, it will become a community-building activity as well.

Note to teachers

Most children enthusiastically respond and begin to dance without needing much encouragement. However, don't be surprised if not all of them do. It may take a while for some children to feel comfortable enough to move around. We have found that even the ones who are hesitant will begin to create movements and dances after becoming more familiar with the music.

Reasons to repeat the same piece of music many times:

- As the children learn the music and get comfortable with it, they come to know what to expect. Then they can plan out their moves to fit with the music.

- Children gradually become more confident and that self-confidence helps them to experience the music on a higher level.

- If you begin each day dancing to the same song, for example, you will find that children will experiment and develop signature movements, their own choreographed dance steps.

- Children will watch each other and try out each other's ideas.

- They will become aware of different instruments and melody lines.

- They will improvise and learn a lot about the music and dance through experimentation and play.

Note: Sometimes adults worry that children will become bored with music they hear repeated day after day. In fact, the opposite is true. Children are excited when they recognize the first few bars of a tune they know and love. It gives them the familiarity they need to respond in an uninhibited way to the music.

Songs by other artists that are great for dancing:

- Count Basie: "One O'Clock Jump"; "Basie Boogie"; "Dance of the Gremlins"; "Corner Pocket"; "Flight of the Foo Birds"; "Shiny Stockings"

- Ella Fitzgerald: "Take the A Train"

- Duke Ellington: "Take the A Train"

- Scott Joplin: "Maple Leaf Rag"

- Peanuts Hucko and Alex Walsh & his Band: "Stealing Apples"

- Chick Webb and His Orchestra: "Stompin' at the Savoy"

For additional song suggestions, please see the Appendix.

Extensions

1.) Teachers can reinforce dance steps that children improvise by observing them and trying them out themselves. You can learn a lot about children's learning strategies as you watch them dance. By incorporating the movement ideas that the children devise, into the curriculum, the music curriculum expands in an organic, meaningful way:

- Teacher observes child.

- Teacher tries out child's dance move.

- Other children watch the teacher and try out the dance idea too.

2.) The children can form a circle, and one by one go into the center of the circle to dance. The others can watch, keep the beat by clapping, or dance along incorporating the child's ideas into their own dancing.

3.) Ask if anyone has a new idea to try out. Then everyone in the room can try it out, too.

4.) Put some of the dance movement ideas together and choreograph a class dance.

5.) Offer shakers or maracas for the children to play as they dance. Other instruments you might want to try are drums, finger cymbals, and tambourines.

Exercising to Recorded Music

Another easy way to add music to your day is to exercise to music. Morning calisthenics are a time-honored tradition. Taking a break from work with exercises has proved to be a valuable tool to improve the quality of workers' production in factories. Exercising to music can stimulate children's brains as they move their limbs. Why not add a little jazz to get things moving?

Materials needed: Recorded music. For suggestions see the Free Dance section and the Appendix.

Procedure

- Put on some recorded music and ask the children to watch you and do what you do.

- Start by clapping your hands and marching in place. Raise your arms over your head and bring them back down in time to the music. Bend forward and come back up. Twist from the waist. The important thing is not which exact movements you choose. Almost any will do.

- Do not change too rapidly from one movement to the next. You are not trying to trick children, such as in a Simon Says game. You want them to be able to get the movements right both for physical safety and musical knowledge.

- You should keep repeating a movement for about four bars before moving on to another.

- Try to group movements together to make patterns. For example, reach your arms up and bring them back down. Then reach out with your arms and bring them back in, then repeat. Children should be able to grasp the pattern and predict which movement will come next. Then add a third movement to the sequence, etc.

- The movements must fit the music so that the rhythm of the music is reinforced by the movements.

- It is sometimes useful to call out the movement as you progress, especially when you are first introducing this activity. "Arms up!" or "Up, down, up, down."

Adding Recorded Music and Movement to Literature

Music and movement can be added to many children's stories. Take the example of Maurice Sendak's *Where the Wild Things Are*. The plot revolves around Max, a small boy who gets in big trouble for various actions such as chasing the family dog with a fork. He is costumed in a wolf suit and his mother calls him "Wild Thing," and banishes him to his bedroom without any supper. Max's room slowly turns into forest and Max sets off by boat to where the wild things are. The wild things are delighted and make Max their king. "King" Max declares that a wild rumpus should start and in the next several pages there is no text, just illustrations showing the wild things cavorting about.

The wild rumpus is a perfect literary situation for fast paced swing music. The children can pretend to be the wild things as they move to the music. Benny Goodman's "Sing Sing Sing" is a perfect vehicle, primarily because of the incredible extended drumming improvisations by Gene Krupa. The children are transported by the music to where the wild things are and joyously join in with the character Max as they become part of the wild rumpus.

You can use the music if you are acting out the entire book, or you can act out just that section of the book. It works well either way. When the music is over, you can continue the story, or you can stop the music before it is finished by having Max yell, "Now stop," as he does in the story.

Extensions

- Offer shakers and drums to the children so they can play along with Gene Krupa.

- Add music to other sections of the book. "Sing Sing Sing" can be used when Max is running around his house at the beginning of the story, causing trouble. A blues song or Duke Ellington's "Solitude" can be played when he is sent to his room without his supper.

Drawing and Painting to Recorded Music
Jackson Pollock (1912–1956).

The famous abstract expressionist painter, Jackson Pollock liked to listen to jazz while he painted. Pollock's style of painting is usually described as action or "drip" painting in which paint is dripped or splattered rather than carefully brushed on. He often would put the canvas on the floor so he could approach the canvas from all sides and angles, much in the way that Native American sand painters did. He would walk around the painting splattering, flinging and dripping paint as he moved. The movements that he made to the music made the painting what it was. Young children can experience the joy of becoming totally involved in creating art within a musical framework in a similar way. Their movements to the music will help create the painting.

Tell the class a little bit about Jackson Pollock. Be sure to mention:

- Jackson Pollock was an abstract expressionist painter.

- His style of painting was called action or "drip" painting because he dripped or splattered the paint instead of carefully brushing it on.

- Sometimes he put his canvases on the floor so that he could walk around them as he painted.

- He often listened to jazz while he painted.

Materials Needed

- Reproductions or images of some of Jackson Pollock's paintings.

- Watered down poster paint so that it is fluid enough to drip from a brush or stick. You can provide primary colors, white and black, or let the children experiment with mixing secondary colors.

- A large canvas or paper that can be placed or taped onto the floor. Poster paint can easily be removed from the floor with a damp mop. However, you can put down a large piece of plastic or newspaper to protect the floor if you desire.

- Various size artists brushes, sticks, and eyedroppers.

- Smocks to cover clothing—this is a very messy project.

- A recording of Benny Goodman's "Sing Sing Sing."

Procedure

- Show the class some reproductions of Pollock's paintings. Some children may have seen his work in a museum.

- Play the music and pantomime drip painting as you move around the canvas or paper, pretending to create your masterpiece.

- Dip a brush into the paint to demonstrate how easily it drips off the brush. Explain that you do not touch the brush to the canvas.

- Choose one or two children to begin. Have each child choose one color. Start the music and let them create. Encourage them to keep moving around the canvas as they apply the paint.

- After a few minutes, choose two new children to take over. Let everyone have one or more turns. As each child adds a color, a Pollock-like painting will begin to appear.

Variations

- Have a canvas for each child so they can create individual works of art.

- Experiment with other pieces of music. Do particular pieces change the movements and therefore what you see in the visual art? Here are some selections you could try from Jackson Pollock's own record collection:

Louis Armstrong, "Mahogany Hall Stomp"

Count Basie, "Boogie Woogie"; "One O'Clock Jump"

Duke Ellington, "Delta Serenade"

Lionel Hampton, "Central Avenue Breakdown"

Coleman Hawkins, "Mop Mop"

Note to Teachers: We like to model how the art projects are done before the children attempt the projects. We think that they are free form enough that the children will not try to copy our results exactly. In our experience, most children have never had this sort of art experience before, so they feel more comfortable with it when they see a visual explanation of the steps involved.

Chapter 7

Latin Jazz — Tito Puente

"If there is no dance there is not music." Tito Puente

JAZZ GREAT—Tito Puente (1923–2000)

Ernesto Antonio Puente, Jr. was called Ernestito (little Ernest) by his family. It was eventually shortened to "Tito." He was born on April 20, 1923 in New York City to immigrant parents from Puerto Rico. When he was a boy, he loved to dance. He also took piano lessons. But when he heard Benny Goodman's band, he fell in love with Gene Krupa's drumming and decided he wanted to become a drummer.

When he was only 13 years old, he became a professional musician. After playing with the famous Machito Orchestra, the first to combine Afro-Cuban and big band music, Tito was drafted into the army.

After World War II ended, Tito returned to New York City and attended the Julliard School of Music. Then in 1948, he established his own Tito Puente Orchestra. He became a sensation.

In the 1950s, he began to record his music and released many hits starting with the best-selling album, *Dance Mania*. Tito Puente had a long career, appearing on television, in the movies, and performing with many of the greatest latin and jazz musicians and jazz legends. He was known as "The King of the Timbales," "The King of Latin Jazz."

Tito Puente Teaching Suggestions

Tell the class a little bit about Tito Puente. Be sure to mention:

- Tito Puente played latin jazz.
- Tito played the timbales, a kind of Cuban drum, and loved to dance.
- His real name was Ernesto but his family called him Ernestito (little Ernesto in Spanish) and eventually shortened it to Tito.
- He had his own orchestra and was famous for playing the mambo.

Latin Jazz

Latin Jazz entered the jazz world in the 1930's and became more popular in the 1940's, 1950's and 1960's. Latin jazz is a style of music that combines the rhythms and instruments from many places including Cuba, Puerto Rico, and Brazil. The Latin dance rhythms of the mambo, cha-cha-cha, samba, and bossa nova influenced many jazz musicians. There are several latin percussion instruments that help create the exciting sound of this music, including conga, bongo, timbales, claves, guiros, and cowbells.

Movement and Dance

One of the simplest and most effective ways to add musical experiences to a child's day is to play recorded music and allow children the opportunity to respond to the music through movement or dance. It is a wonderful way to begin the day, transition to a subject area or begin an art or music lesson. Tito Puente recorded an enormous number of dance tunes which young children respond to in a positive and enthusiastic way.

Free Dance

Materials needed: Recorded music. Below are a few Tito Puente songs that are great for dancing.

- "El Rey del Timbal"

- "Mambo La Roca"

- "New Arrival"

Procedure

- Put on recorded music and listen to it for awhile.

- Encourage the children to move to the rhythms they hear while seated.

- Encourage the children to stand up and move around to the music.

- If all of the adults in the room dance with the children, it will become a community—building activity as well.

Note to Teachers: Most children enthusiastically respond and begin to dance without needing much encouragement. However, don't be surprised if not all of them do. It may take a while for some children to feel comfortable enough to move around. We have found that even the ones who are hesitant will begin to create movements and dances after becoming more familiar with the music.

Reasons to repeat the same piece of music many times:

- As the children learn the music and get comfortable with it, they come to know what to expect. Then they can plan out their moves to fit with the music.

- Children gradually become more confident, and that self-confidence helps them to experience the music on a higher level.

- If you begin each day dancing to the same song, for example, you will find that children will experiment and develop signature movements, their own choreographed dance steps.

- Children will watch each other and try out each other's ideas.

- They will become aware of different instruments and melody lines.

- They will improvise and learn a lot about the music and dance through experimentation and play.

Note

Sometimes adults worry that children will become bored with music they hear repeated day after day. In fact, the opposite is true. Children are excited when they recognize the first few bars of a tune they know and love. It gives them the familiarity they need to respond in an uninhibited way to the music.

Mambos by other artists that are great for dancing:

"Mambo Italiano" by various artists, such as Dean Martin and Rosemary Clooney.

"Mambo I, I ,I" by Sesame Street.

"El Cumbanchero" by various artists, such as Desi Arnaz, Perez Prado and Celia Cruz.

Extensions

- Teachers can reinforce dance steps that children improvise by observing them and trying them out themselves. You can learn a lot about children's learning strategies as you watch them dance. By incorporating the movement ideas that the children devise, into the curriculum, the music curriculum expands in an organic, meaningful way:

- Teacher observes child.

- Teacher tries out child's dance move.

- Other children watch the teacher and try out the dance idea, too.

- The children can form a circle and one by one go into the center of the circle to dance. The others can watch, keep the beat by clapping, or dance along incorporating the child's ideas into their own dancing.

- Ask if anyone has a new idea to try out. Then everyone in the room can try it out, too.

- Put some of the dance movement ideas together and choreograph a class dance.

- Offer shakers or maracas for the children to play as they dance. Other instruments you might want to try are drums, finger cymbals and tambourines.

Structured Dance—The Mambo

Tito Puente was widely known as the King of the Mambo. Although the mambo is a little too challenging for most young children to learn, a modified version can be a lot of fun for them to master. "Mambo La Roca" is a good song to try. The beat is fast but you can do it in half time.

1. Place your right foot forward leaving the left foot in place.

2. Rock back and forth—R,L,R,L

3. Bring your right foot back.

4. Place your left foot forward leaving the right foot in place.

5. Rock back and forth—L,R,L,R

6. Bring your left foot back.

7. Stand in place and wiggle your hips from side to side.

Extension

Adding maracas: Tito Puente loved to dance while he played his timbales. Children can also experience the joy of playing an instrument and dancing by playing maracas as they mambo. Do the structured dance steps that you taught them and add a free dance section where kids can improvise to the mambo beat as they play their maracas.

Exercising to Recorded Music

Another easy way to add music to your day is to exercise to music. Morning calisthenics are a time-honored tradition. Taking a break from work with exercises has proved to be a valuable tool to improve the quality of workers' production in factories. Exercising to music can stimulate children's brains as they move their limbs. Why not add a little jazz to get things moving?

Materials needed: Recorded music. For suggestions see the Free Dance section and the appendix.

Procedure:

- Put on some recorded music and ask the children to watch you and do what you do.

- Start by clapping your hands and marching in place. Raise your arms over your head and bring them back down in time to the music. Bend forward and come back up. Twist from the waist. Choose any movements you like. Almost any will do.

- Do not change too rapidly from one movement to the next. You are not trying to trick children such as in a Simon Says game. You want them to be able to get the movements right both for physical safety and musical knowledge.

- You should keep repeating a movement for about four bars before moving on to another.

- Try to group movements together to make patterns. For example, reach your arms up and bring them back down. Then reach out with your arms and bring them back in. Then repeat. Children should be able to grasp the pattern and predict which movement will come next. Then add a third movement to the sequence, etc.

- The movements must fit the music so that the rhythm of the music is reinforced by the movements. Wiggle your hips to the latin beat.

- It is sometimes useful to call out the movement as you progress especially when you are first introducing this activity. "Arms up!" or "Up, down, up, down."

Mambo Art: Drawing and Painting to Recorded Music
Materials needed

- recorded music by Tito Puente

- maracas or shakers

- drawing paper

- washable markers in bright color

Procedure

- Play "Mambo La Roca" or a similar mambo by Tito Puente. Play the maracas for the children as they listen to the song.

- Pass out maracas and let the children improvise to the mambo music.

- After the children are thoroughly familiar with the music and have had ample opportunity to experiment with the maracas have them sit down at tables and give them drawing paper. Then play the mambo again, suggesting that they pretend that the maracas are "dancing" on the paper.

- Next collect the maracas and hand out washable markers. Use the brightest colors that are available. Ask the children to hold one marker in each hand as they did with the maracas. Now play the music again instructing the children to let the markers "dance" on the paper in the same way that the maracas did. As the markers mambo across the drawing paper a work of art which incorporates the movement of the mambo will be created.

Variations
- Mambo mural: Using a roll of paper large enough for several children to use at the same time, make a mambo mural.

- Vary paper sizes from small to large.

- Try using different size markers, crayons, finger paint and poster paints with different size brushes.

Note to Teachers

We like to model how the art projects are done before the children attempt the projects. We think that they are free form enough that the children will not try to copy our results exactly. In our experience, most children have never had this sort of art experience before, so they feel more comfortable with it when they see a visual explanation of the steps involved.

Craft Project: Make Percussion Instruments

Latin jazz uses many different kinds of percussion instruments which add a variety of sounds to the music. This craft project is designed to construct shakers which will make a variety of sounds.

Materials needed

- Small plastic drinking cups

- Masking tape in bright colors

- Assorted filler materials such as sand, rice, beans, pebbles, washers, small jingle bells

- Spoons for each material.

- Materials for decorating the outside of the cups such as markers and stickers

- Sample shakers, each containing one of the filler materials.

Procedure

- Show the children the already assembled shaker and shake each one for them, noting the different sounds they make.

- Explain the steps that the children will follow to make their own shakers.

- Give each child two cups.

- Allow each child to select a filler material and fill one of the cups no more than 1/4 full. You can draw a line on each cup to help guide them if desired.

- Turn the second cup upside down and place on top of the first cup. Let the child choose a colored tape. With help from an adult, tape the two cups together with masking tape. Be careful to run the tape all the way around the lips of the cups so that they are sealed tightly together.

- Decorate the outside of the cup as desired.

- Test each shaker and listen to the sound it makes.

- Experiment with each other's shakers, comparing the sounds.

Extensions

- Have each child make four different shakers, each with a different filling.

- Try to guess which filling is in each shaker by listening to the sound each makes.

- Which is the loudest shaker? Which shaker has the lowest tone?

- Experiment with playing with the various shakers while playing a Tito Puente song.

Chapter 8

The Blues — Taj Majal

"Through active participation in different styles of blues music, children discover the historical, cultural, and artistic features of this music."
The Wolf Trap Institute for Early Learning

JAZZ GREAT—*Taj Majal (1942–)*

Taj Mahal's birth name was Henry Saint Clair Fredericks. He was born into a musical family on May 17, 1942 in New York City. His father played jazz piano and composed and arranged music and his mother sang in a gospel choir. He spent most of his childhood living in Springfield, Massachusetts, where musicians from all over the United States, the Caribbean and Africa often visited his family. Because of this early exposure to a variety of musical styles, Taj has always been interested in music from around the world.

As a young boy Taj took piano, trombone and harmonica lessons. When he was 13 he learned how to play acoustic blues guitar. He studied agriculture in college, planning to become a farmer, but his great love of music made him change his mind after college and he decided to become a musician instead.

His fascination with India one day inspired him to dream about India's *Taj Majal*, one of the most beautiful buildings in the world. When he awoke, he decided to change his name to Taj Majal and has used that name ever since.

Taj Majal has recorded many albums and even some blues songs just for children! You can enjoy many of them on his *Shake Sugaree* album.

Taj Majal Teaching Suggestions

Tell the class a little bit about Taj Majal. Be sure to mention:

- Taj Majal sings the blues.

- He plays the blues guitar.

- His real name is Henry St. Clair Fredericks but one night he dreamed of the beautiful Taj Majal building in India and decided to change his name to Taj Majal.

- He recorded many blues songs and even made some just for children.

The Funky Bluesy ABCs

- Play The "Funky Bluesy ABC's" from the *Shake Sugaree* album.

- Lead the children in movements that identify the beat of the song: pat legs; sway hips; wave arms in the air; tap foot; shake hands in the air; move shoulders; etc.

- Hand out shakers and lead the activity again.

- Ask for a volunteer(s) to be the leader.

> **Note to Teachers:** Finding appropriate blues songs and artists for young children can be somewhat challenging. Pay close attention to the lyrics before sharing songs with the children.

About the Blues

The blues evolved from African-American work songs, field hollers, spirituals and country string ballads in the late 1800's. It is an American musical form and is the foundation of jazz, rhythm and blues, rock and roll and even hip hop music. See Appendix for more information on the harmonic structure of the blues.

The blues and young children may seem an unlikely combination. Blues songs are usually associated with adults who are down and out or unlucky in love. We empathize with the feelings expressed by the blues singer because we all have had similar experiences. However, blues music isn't always about sadness. As the great blues singer Alberta Hunter said, "The blues is about truth-telling." Blues songs tell stories about feelings. These stories could be about something that happened today, yesterday, last week, or years ago. The storytelling nature of the blues makes it a natural fit for the early childhood classroom. Singing the blues doesn't change the situation, but it does seem to make the children feel a whole lot better. Expressing our feelings and telling our stories through song with other people, gives us support and connects us to a community.

The Blues—Teaching Suggestions

Tell the class a little bit about the Blues. Be sure to mention:

- Blues songs tell stories about feelings.

- Singing the blues makes you feel better.

- The Blues is an American musical form.

- Everybody gets the blues sometimes.

"What Did You Have For Breakfast?"

This song is a great example of the storytelling nature of the blues. It is a simple and non-threatening way to get started. It asks the children to share what they had for breakfast with the classroom community. The "chorus" line, "What did you have for breakfast" can be stated by the teacher or the whole group together. The easy-to-grasp pattern of the song: Question—Answer—Question—Answer is satisfying to young children. It is also easy for the teacher to insert prompts for children who have trouble remembering what they had for breakfast. It can also be fun to make up answers!

What Did You Have For Breakfast?

Louise Rogers

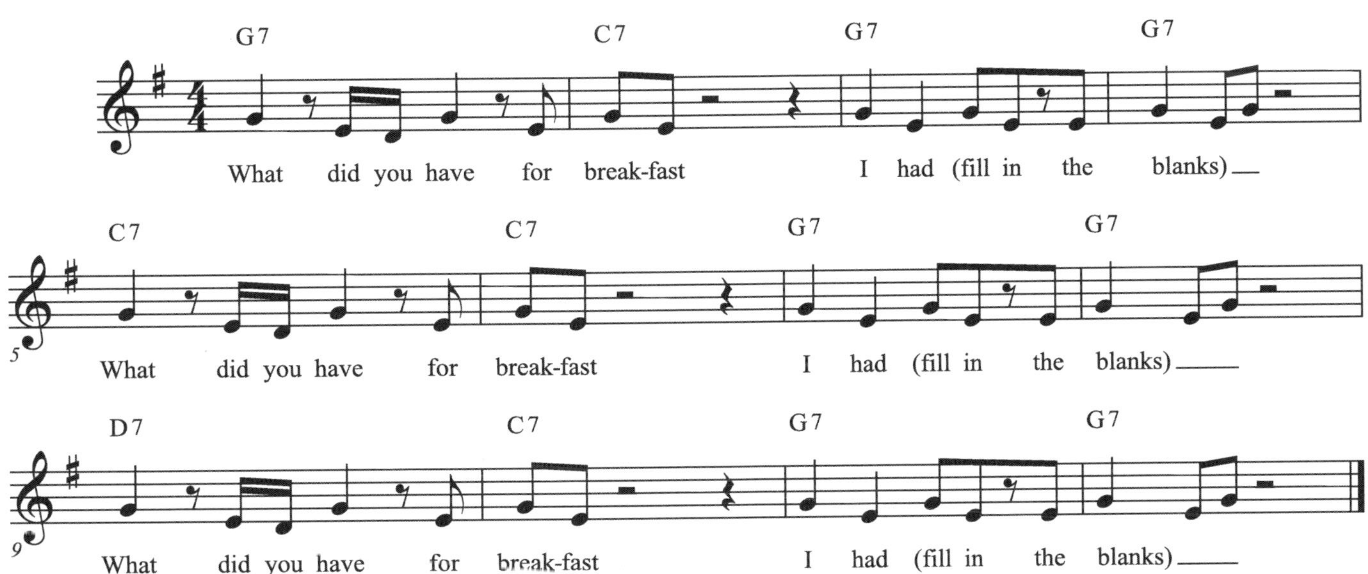

Teaching Suggestion: *What Did You Have For Breakfast?*

- Tell the class that they are going to hear a blues song about breakfast.

- Ask the class what they had for breakfast.

- Listen to the song on the CD.

- Encourage the class to discuss what they heard.

- Tell the children they will each have an opportunity to speak or sing their answer as the class asks the question "What did you have for breakfast?" This is a form of call and response. The call is the question. The response is different each time as the children answer the question.

- Lead the class by asking the musical question "What did you have for breakfast?" Encourage them to join you in singing the question and let your voice and body be animated.

- Feel free to improvise by asking questions or making comments before leading the group in the next repetition of the question.

- When you are confident that the class knows the song, play *Rick's Blues, Slow Blues in G* by Jamie Aebersold, or your own accompaniment on the piano, autoharp, or guitar, etc., and sing the song with the children. See written music for chords and melody.

Example

Question (asked in unison by the whole group led by the teacher): *What did you have for breakfast?*

Answer: *I had eggs for breakfast.*

Question: *Were they scrambled?*

Answer: *No, fried.*

Question: *Did you have toast too?*

Answer: *I had toast and a cup of juice.*

Extensions

- What did you have for lunch? Dinner? Snack?

- What do animals have for breakfast?

- Nutrition—What are healthful foods?

- Cultural differences—What do people in other areas of the world eat for breakfast?

- Math Activity—Create a graph of the children's favorite foods.

Animal Blues

Louise Rogers

The repetitive nature of this blues song makes it easy to learn. It uses scatting to help tell a simple story. Scatting is a jazz language used by singers to try to make their voices sound like musical instruments. When you are scatting you are playing with sounds and creating new melodies and/or rhythms.

The song first introduces the farmer who loves his farm "way up on the hill." After announcing that the farm "gives to him a thrill," he expresses his joy through scatting. In turn, each of the animals on the farm repeats the farmer's sentiments and scats in its own language. It is fun to sing along with the recording. When the class is comfortable with the song, sing it without the recording adding as many animals as you desire. Have fun figuring out how each would scat. If you are uncomfortable singing, try chanting it. Be expressive with your voice.

Teaching Suggestions

- Add clapping or drumming to help keep a beat.

- Pretend to be each animal.

- Explore dynamics (loud and soft). For example, make the cow scat softly and get louder.

- Substitute a new environment for the farm. For example, "I have a rain forest way up on a hill" or "I have a city way up on a hill" or "I have a pond way up on a hill."

- Phonics—Write down the scat sounds of each animal.

The Talking Blues

The talking blues is a great form for teachers who are uncomfortable with their singing voices. The lyrics are spoken rather than sung and the fixed rhythm makes it easier to insert an original line or tell an original story. Chris Bouchillon is believed to be the founder of the talking blues in the 1920's. Many well-known musicians such as Woody Guthrie, Bob Marley and Bob Dylan, have used the talking blues form to tell stories.

An easy way to explore the talking blues is by reading a book to a blues accompaniment. You can use *Rick's Blues* on the CD, *Slow Blues in G* by Jamie Aebersold, or any instrumental blues song. *Alexander and the Terrible, Horrible, No Good, Very Bad Day* is a book that we find works very well. It contains many situations with which the children will easily identify.

Teaching Suggestion: *Alexander and the Terrible, Horrible, No Good, Very Bad Day* by Judith Viorst

- Read the book aloud to the class with the blues music on in the background.

- Have a class discussion about the things that upset Alexander and make a list for the class to see.

- Introduce the idea of turning those bad feelings into music—the blues.

- Discuss some of the things that give the children the blues and make a list, if desired.

- Play the blues music again but this time read the list that the children compiled to the music.

Extension: Create an Original Blues

Write a blues song using some of the ideas from the class's blues list. They can create their own blues verses, and/or create a blues song that fits with the story of Alexander and his terrible day.

Sample verse

Tell the class to start with "I woke up this morning" Ask them to finish the sentence. What happened next? Use an idea from the list that the class created.

I woke up this morning—my mama left me at school
(this line always repeats)
I woke up this morning—my mama left me at school
(The last word of the next phrase should rhyme with last word of the phrase before which was "school". Help the class to finish the phrase.)
She left me at school—I want to go the pool!

The class sings/chants:

I woke up this morning—my mama left me at school
I woke up this morning—my mama left me at school
She left me at school—I want to go to the pool!

Miss My Mama Blues

It occurred to us one day, while observing a young child crying after his mother dropped him off at our nursery school, that this child might benefit by singing the blues. The little boy knew that his mother would come back for him. He knew that his teachers would take good care of him. He even knew that soon he would have fun laughing and playing with his friends at school. But right at that moment, all he could think about was his mother, and how much he wanted her to be with him.

It seemed like the right time and place for a blues song. Thus, the "Miss My Mama Blues" was born. It's a simple song that we sing with the children when they are missing their mommies (or daddies, grandparents, or other caregivers, etc.).

I've got the miss my mama blues
I've got the miss my mama blues
I've got the Miss my mama
Got the miss my Mama
Got the miss my mama blues.

Miss My Mama Blues

"Miss My Mama Blues" can be found in our "Three Little Jazzy Pigs" story in *Jazzy Fairy Tales*. The pigs sing it because they miss their mama. (*Jazzy Fairy Tales* is available through Alfred Music Publishing and www.jazzyfairytales.com.)

Louise Rogers

Chapter 9

Jazz Poetry

Children's Poet Eve Merriam (1916–1992)

"…a good poem contains both meaning and music.
Whatever you do, find ways to read poetry.
Eat it, drink it, enjoy it, and share it."
Eve Merriam

Eve Merriam was born in Philadelphia on July 19, 1916. Her given name was Eva Moscovitz. She always enjoyed reading and writing poetry. She often was taken to the theater by her family and she particularly loved the rhythms and rhymes in the operettas of Gilbert and Sullivan. She graduated from the University of Pennsylvania and then moved to New York City where she became a writer. Although she also wrote books and plays for adults, she was first and foremost a writer of poetry for children.

"I find it difficult to sit still when I hear poetry or read it out loud. I feel a tingling feeling all over, particularly in the tips of my fingers and in my toes, and it just seems to go right from my mouth all the way through my body. It's like a shot of adrenalin or oxygen when I hear rhymes and word play," Eve Merriam to Glenna Sloan in *Language Arts, 1981.*

In this chapter we have not highlighted a jazz great, but the great children's poet, Eve Merriam. It is widely acknowledged that music and poetry have a lot in common. Here one of Eve Merriam's poems, "Crusty Cornbread," is explored using jazz. This is not a new idea. In fact, in the 1920's jazz and poetry were both evolving as artists experimented with rhythm and improvisation. Some poets and Bebop musicians worked together, listening and sharing elements of jazz such as swing, syncopation and improvisation. Joining jazz and poetry together in the classroom can be an exciting learning experience.

Eve Merriam Teaching Suggestions

Tell the class a little bit about Eve Merriam. Be sure to mention:

- Eve Merriam was born in Philadelphia, Pennsylvania.

- Her real name was Eva Moscovitz.

- She loved the musical theater, especially Gilbert and Sullivan.

- She was first and foremost a writer of poetry for children.

Note to Teachers

Explain to the students that they will be listening to a piece called "Crusty Cornbread" and that it is comprised of three parts. Listen to the recording (track #) before playing it for the class so that you are familiar with it and will be able to help the children recognize the different parts. In the first part, the poem is read. (We refer to this as the A Section.)

The second part is in the form of a question/answer. The question is comprised of notes played by an acoustic bass. The first answer to the question on the recording is three snaps. This question/answer is repeated three times. The second answer to the question is three claps. This question/answer is also repeated three times. (We refer to this as the B Section.)

The third part is a solo section with the voice scatting. The singer sings made-up words and a made-up melody. (We refer to this as the C section. The form of the piece is as follows: ABABC...ABAB.) Now, play the piece for the class and help them identify each part. The piece is short and moves quickly. You will need to play the recording several times in order for the children to be comfortable identifying the patterns.

"Crusty Cornbread:" Track #1, poem by Eve Merriam from the book *You be Good, I'll be Night*.

The Poem
Crusty cornbread

Crumbly crumbs

Mumbly muffins

Buttery thumbs

Flakey biscuits

Crunchy toast

Cracks in the crackers

Crumble the most

Teaching the A section: The Poem

- Recite the entire poem and have the children echo back line by line.

Teacher: Crusty cornbread	Teacher: Flakey biscuits
Class: Crusty cornbread	Class: Flakey biscuits
Teacher: Crumbly crumbs	Teacher: Crunchy toast
Class: Crumbly crumbs	Class: Crunchy toast
Teacher: Mumbly muffins	Teacher: Cracks in the crackers
Class: Mumbly muffins	Class: Cracks in the crackers
Teacher: Buttery thumbs	Teacher: Crumble the most
Class: Buttery thumbs	Class: Crumble the most

- Now say the poem all together several times, with no echoing.

Teaching the B section: Question/Answer section

Question/Answer: In this piece, the question does not consist of words but instead is comprised of notes played on an acoustic bass. The question/answer format is used to generate creative responses to a repeated question. The question remains the same each time. The "answer" on the recording is three snaps the first time and three claps the second time. In this case, the "answer" happens to be the same rhythmic pattern both times. However, in the following activities, children should be encouraged to create and experiment with different rhythmic patterns.

Note to teachers: To get the class started, we suggest that you begin with a real question. For example, "What's your rhythm?" The question is always the same, but everyone will have a different answer. The children will play the answer back as rhythmic patterns which will vary. See written music and/or listen to the recording, track #

Question—Rhythm

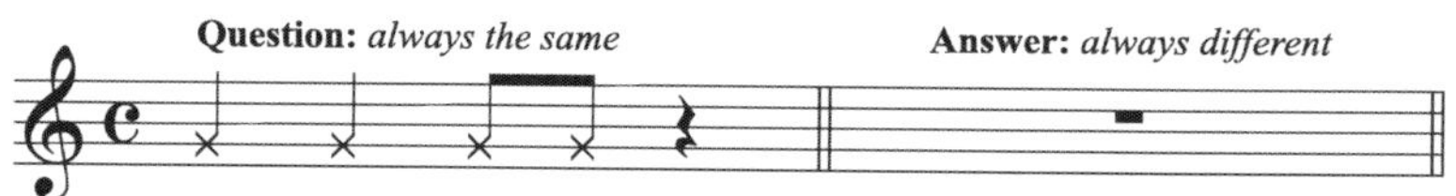

- Have the class sit in a circle.

- Teacher asks the question, "What's your rhythm?" or "How's that cornbread?"

- Students can "answer" the question with a rhythmic pattern on the body such as:

  Claps

  Tap your knees, shoulders, feet, head, etc.

  Roll your arms

  Snap your fingers

  Stomp your feet

- Or students can answer with a simple percussion instrument such as:

  Rhythm sticks

  Drums

  Shakers

  Bells

  Guiros

- Now, instead of speaking the question with words, the teacher plays the "question" with an instrument of choice.

- See above list of percussion instruments

  See the written music for the actual rhythmic notation for the question. However, feel free to create your own rhythm for the question. The practice questions, "What's your rhythm?" and "How's that cornbread?" fit perfectly with this rhythm.

Using Pitched Instruments for the Question

Playing the question with a pitched instrument (an instrument with notes) is fun. This is how it is done on the recording. The string bass asks the question and it is answered with a rhythmic response. Using a pitched instrument, the question can be asked by using approximate pitches, such as low, medium, high, or the question can be played by using the actual pitches.

Suggestions

- Talking drum notes (low, medium, high)

- Tubano drum (low, low, high)

- Resonator bars (see written music)

- Glockenspiel (see written music)

- Xylophone (see written music)

- Piano (see written music)

C section—Improvised Vocal Solos (scat)

Scat: "Scat" is a jazz language used by vocalists when trying to make their voices sound like instruments. The singer sings made-up words and a made-up melody that "fit" or sound good over the chords of the piece. When you are scatting you are playing with sounds, which is an age appropriate literacy and music activity for young children and a whole lot of fun.

Whether you are singing or speaking your scat phrases, we encourage you to explore your voice and have fun! Adding some of the following musical elements will help to make your scat phrases more interesting and diverse:

- Dynamics—the loudness or softness of your voice.

- Crescendos—allowing your voice to slowly get louder.

- Decrescendos—allowing your voice to slowly get softer.

- Slides—sliding your voice from one note to another.

- Rests—allowing pauses in your scat phrases.

- Inflection—changing the tone or pitch of your voice while either speaking or singing. This happens naturally as we speak. We do not speak in a monotone. For example, when we ask a question our voice usually goes up in pitch at the end of the sentence.

- High voice and low voice—changing out of your natural register. How high can you go? How low can you go? Experiment.

- Rhythmic Diversity—long words and short words.

- Patterns—creating rhythmic and or melodic patterns.

- Syncopation— A syncopated rhythm is one that delivers an element of rhythmic surprise.

It is easy to teach scatting by echoing. This is different from the recording. However, the concept is to give the students ideas that they can work with as they become more comfortable with their scatting abilities.

- Refer to the written music for scatting ideas and feel free to create new ones of your own. The written music includes the instrumental question.

- Playing the melodic riff in between the scat phrases will help to keep the tonality of the piece (G mixolydian).

- Sing the scat phrase and have the class be your echo. *If you are uncomfortable singing, it is fine to use the voice to create rhythmic scatting.*

- Be sure to ask for soloists! Some kids will enjoy singing solo while others will want to remain as part of the group

Scat Section — Echo

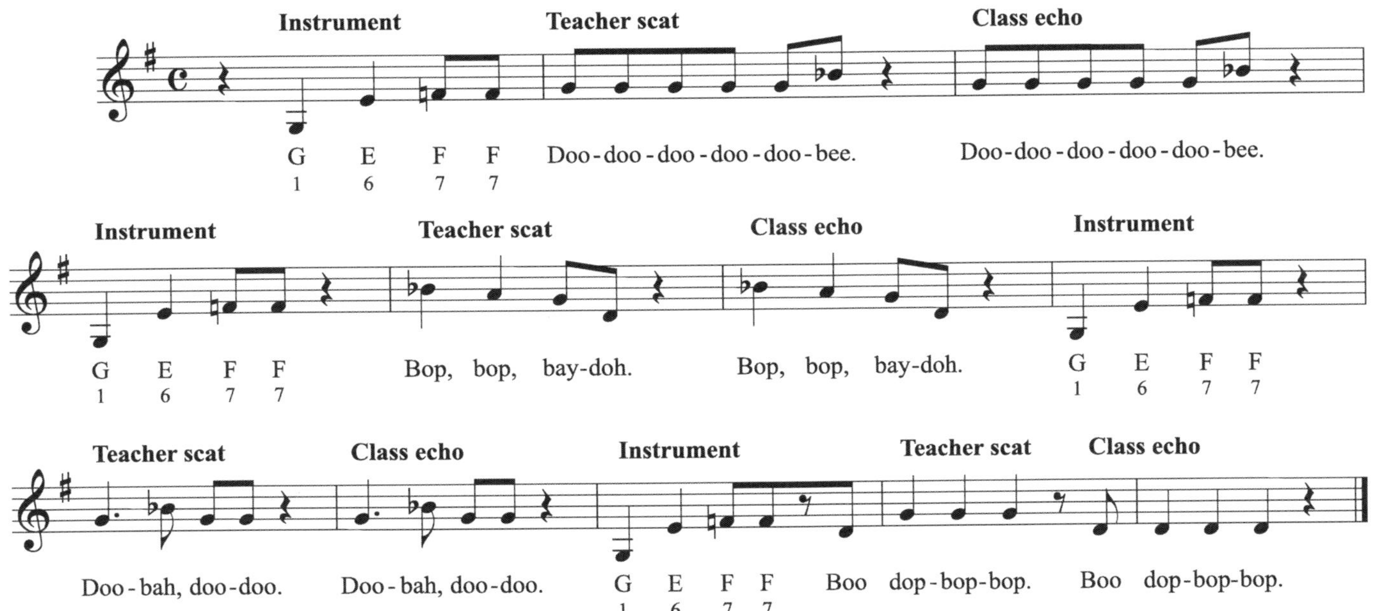

Putting it All Together!

Now, you have all you need in order to create your own version of Crusty Cornbread.

Form

The form on the recording is ABABC... ABABAB. However, have fun creating your own form. For example, ABBBBBABBBBC... ABABAB.

A section

Teacher/class recites poem—use dynamics, rhythm and inflection to create excitement, energy and swing.

B Section

Decide on the question: Will it be spoken? Will it be played on an instrument? Will it be sung?

Decide how many answers to the question you will have. Who will answer these questions?

Or perhaps have the answer be different every time.

C Section

Decide if there will be soloists or if everyone will have a chance to scat.

It can be fun to record it and have the class listen for the different sections: the patterns; the questions/answers; and the scats.

Extensions/Variations

A Section:

Shakers can be added during the poem. I suggest one shaker per student and they clap with it creating a very clear rhythm for accompaniment.

Teacher can add an accompaniment by playing the drum on beats 2 and 4. This creates a nice ensemble.

Try this with another poem, nursery rhyme or make up one of your own.

B Section:

One hand drum per student. Students can create rhythmic responses on the drums.

Students can create vocal responses instead of rhythmic responses.

C Section:

Perform rhythmically inspired improvisation solos on drums instead of vocal solos (scats).

C Section:

Encourage children to scat their own creative responses.

Extensions into other Curriculum Areas
Literacy skills – phonics:

Find the words which start with the hard C sound. There are a total of eight hard C-words in the song—crusty, cornbread, crumbly, crumbs, cracks, crackers, crunchy, and crumble.

Think of some more words that start with the hard C sound.

Social Studies

What is cornbread and where did it come from?

A thick, unleavened flatbread made from corn was a staple of the diet of Eastern Woodland Indians. Frequently, this bread was cooked in the embers of a fire. The bread soon became a mainstay in the diet of New England and southern colonists, who called it corn pone.

The Iroquois made corn bread from corn flour mixed with boiling water until it formed a stiff paste. The dough was kneaded, shaped into a ball, and then flattened so that it was about an inch and a half thick and about seven inches in diameter. Each piece was put into a pot of boiling water with a special bread paddle. When the cakes were cooked, they were removed from the water. Eaten hot or cold, they were sometimes covered with corn syrup. Because the Indians, and later the colonists, took these loaves with them as they traveled, they were called journey cakes. Eventually the colonists modified them to make what were called johnny-cakes, as well.

Indians living in the Southeast taught colonists to make fried corn bread by dropping spoonfuls of cornmeal dough into hot bear fat to make what became known as hushpuppies.

From: *American Indian Contributions to the World: 15,000 Years of Inventions and Innovations* by Emory Dean Keoke & Kay Marie Porterfield.

Cooking

Prepare some cornbread with your class.
Prep Time: 10 Min
Cook Time: 25 Min
Ready In: 35 Min

Recipe Yield 1–9 inch round pan
Ingredients

- 1 cup all-purpose flour
- 1 cup yellow cornmeal
- 2/3 cup white sugar
- 1 teaspoon salt
- 3 1/2 teaspoons baking powder
- 1 egg
- 1 cup milk
- 1/3 cup vegetable oil

Directions

- Preheat oven to 400 degrees F (200 degrees C). Spray or lightly grease a 9 inch round cake pan.

- In a large bowl, combine flour, cornmeal, sugar, salt and baking powder. Stir in egg, milk and vegetable oil until well combined. Pour batter into prepared pan.

- Nutritional Information

    Amount Per Serving Calories: 188 | Total Fat: 7.4g | Cholesterol: 19mg

A Jazz Festival in Your School or Community

A Jazz Festival is a wonderful way to celebrate the arts with your community. It may take many forms and can be individualized to any school or neighborhood. It could be a one day event, a weekend, a week, or more. It could be interpreted as a theme for any period of time. It could be part of Black History Month or a Multi-Cultural celebration. It could be held during April, Jazz Appreciation Month. The chapters in this book have all you need to know to have a successful Jazz Festival in your school.

Planning

It is a good idea to form a small committee to plan and organize the festival's events. Try to have representatives from the faculty, the administration, and parents to get a wide range of views.

There are several crucial questions for the committee to consider as you begin to plan for your festival.

- How long do you want the festival to last?

- What is your budget for the festival?

- Will it be a one day festival during which normal school schedules will be suspended or a longer festival which will take place within the normal schedule?

- Will you bring in outside paid musicians or rely solely upon the members of your school community?

- Will you broaden the festival to include neighbors, friends and family?

- What are your educational goals for the children?

- How will you help prepare the children to participate in the Festival?

Preparation

In order to spread the workload, allocate jobs to various members of the committee. Some of the responsibilies will include:

- Organizing and scheduling events

- Publicizing the festival through articles in the school newsletter, posters and flyers to parents, etc.

- Finding and organizing paid and volunteer participants—Put out a call for volunteers to families of your children. The volunteers may be jazz instrumentalists or singers or non-musicians who just love jazz and want to share some of their favorite tunes or tell stories about their favorite jazz musicians.

- Look at all of the people and programs on the staff of your school to see how they might fit into and contribute to the jazz festival. Music and art teachers are obvious contributors but you may find teachers who sing or play an instrument or language, movement, science and math teachers who have ideas on how to contribute that you didn't consider.

- Consider any special programs related to jazz that your school usually schedules such as percussionists, dancers, choirs or ensembles and make them part of the festival.

Before the Festival Begins

The committee should meet with all of the classroom teachers to inform them about the jazz festival and to talk with them about what each of them might like to do to contribute to the Festival in their individual rooms. This could encompass a wide range of possibilities including but not limited to:

- Displaying a selection of books about jazz musicians from the classroom library.

- Compiling a selection of recorded jazz music that can be played for the children at transition times, or to dance to over the course of the jazz festival. (See Appendix for suggestions.)

- Making scrapbook albums to make "memory books" for their class with photographs that are taken throughout the festival.

- Using lesson plans found in this book.

- Utilizing the short biographies of jazz greats found in this book.

During The Festival

Each jazz festival will be unique and should be allowed to unfold in its own way. Jazz is improvisational in nature. As the festival goes on, enthusiasm will build and, as the knowledge base develops and expands, new ideas will spring up and more members of the community will join in.

- If possible, take photographs each day and post them in a common area for families to see as well as distribute copies to each classroom for their scrapbooks.

- Monitor the events and troubleshoot any problems that might occur. It can be helpful to assign someone to make sure that all outside contributors are greeted and escorted to their venue and are kept to their time schedule.

Ending the Festival with a Culminating Event

You might want to plan a culminating event such as a dance, concert or a party with refreshments and a display of artwork and photographs created during the festival.

After the Festival

It is a good idea for the committee to meet with the teachers after the festival is over to discuss their experiences and to get suggestions for next year's festival. Try to do this as soon as possible after the festival concludes so that the ideas are fresh in everyone's minds.

We think that you will find that the benefits of having a jazz festival far outweigh the work and expense involved. It is a celebration of music, movement, art and story that ties the community together. It is a joyous multicultural celebration which will delight children, teachers, and parents

A Sample Schedule of Events from a Jazz Festival in a Preschool:

This festival was ten days long. It featured three paid performances, contributions from parents and other family members, science and art projects. Photographs were taken each day and posted on the lobby bulletin boards so that the families could see what was happening during the festival. The culminating event was a performance from the music teacher, an art display of children's projects and a pizza supper enjoyed by children and their families. Here are some of the highlights:

- Rhumbatap—A jazz tap dancer and his piano accompanist.

- Latin Jazz—A pianist and saxophone/flutist duo.

- Percussion—A jazz percussionist/storyteller and his many instruments.

- Senior Center luncheon—Sharing an inter-generational meal to the sounds of a jazz band.

- Jazz stories—True stories of jazz greats and jazzy fairy tales from our school storyteller.

- Parents in the classrooms—Family volunteers playing instruments, reading jazz poetry and telling stories.

- Movement to the swing bands of the big band era—Our movement teacher adds jazz to her curriculum during the festival.

- The science of sound—Explorations of sound and vibration with our science specialist including making percussion instruments.

- Art projects—Splatter painting à la Jackson Pollock to Benny Goodman's big band music; drawing to various jazz selections.

- Language arts—*Charlie Parker Played Bebop* and other jazzy books were read and discussed. (See Appendix for book lists.)

- Final event - Pizza supper, artwork display and performance of a jazzy fairy tale by the music teacher and her accompanist.

- After the festival ended, the photographs were distributed amongst the classrooms so that each class could make a memory book about the festival to keep in their classrooms.

Appendix

This section gives a general overview of the music theory used in *Jazz Mosaic*.

Division of Rhythmic Values

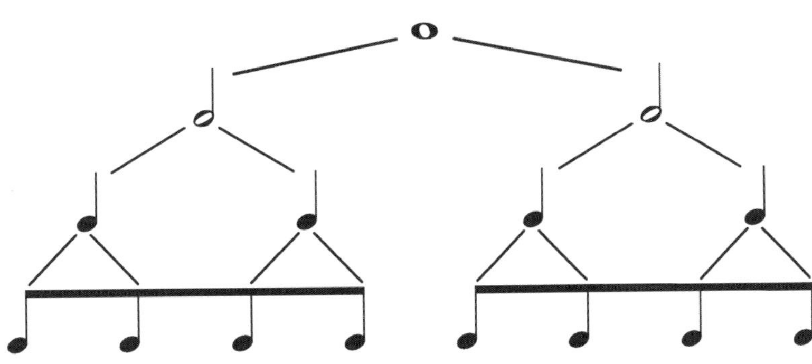

 Whole Note = 4 beats

 Half Note = 2 beats

 Quarter Note = 1 beat

 Two Eighth Notes = 1 beat

A Quarter Note + an Eighth Note—a dot adds half of a beat

Measure or Bar

Groups of notes are divided equally into *measures*. The vertical lines separating these groups are called *bar lines*. The distance between two bar lines is a *bar* or *measure*.

Tempo

The tempo of a piece of music is how fast or slow the pulse of the music is.

Meter

Meter refers to the rhythmic pattern and pulse of groupings of notes. More specifically, it has to do with the strong and weak or accented and unaccented beats. We can subdivide these patterns into groups of two or three beats. Our bodies and our ears naturally feel the pulse of the music and where the accents are. Usually, each measure in the piece has the same number of beats. The meter is indicated by the time signature.

$\frac{4}{4}$ – Also known as quadruple meter and common time

This means that there are 4 beats per measure and a quarter note gets one beat. We feel the pulse in groups of 4 with an accent every 4 beats. We are subconsciously counting 1-2-3-4 in our heads as we listen to the music.

$\frac{3}{4}$ – Also known as triple meter or waltz time

This means that there are 3 beats per measure and that a quarter note gets one beat. We feel the pulse or accent every 3 beats. We are subconsciously counting 1-2-3 in our heads.

Jazz Terminology

Scat

Scat is a jazz language used by singers. Composing a melody on the spot that "fits" or sounds good over the chords of the piece, the singer imitates an instrument (such as the saxophone) by using only their voice and creates made up words such as "beedle-ee-bop." Good scat singers can be very expressive with their voices and at times can convey the message of the song even better without using the real words at all! Scatting should feel and sound natural.

A Little Scat History

Vocal improvisation or scat singing dates back to the early 1900s and possibly even earlier. However, one of the first recorded examples was Louis Armstrong. While recording "The Heebie Jeebies," he dropped the lyrics and began scatting to replace the words. This mix of words and nonsense syllables became quite popular and "Scat Singing" was born. Many singers tried to imitate Louis Armstrong's style of scatting but Ella Fitzgerald was the singer who is credited with having made scat singing a household word. Her scatting was so impeccably clear, her notes were precise and her ear was astounding. She could instantaneously incorporate parts of a Charlie Parker or Dizzy Gillespie solo into her own improvised scat.

Other scat singers include:

- Sarah Vaughn
- Carmen McRae
- Betty Carter
- Mel Torme, Babs Gonzales
- Jon Hendricks
- Al Jarreau
- Kurt Elling
- Bobby McFerrin

Syncopation

Syncopation is when the emphasis is felt on the usually unaccented beats or when there is a shift in accents often creating a rhythmic surprise or a completely different feel—such as swing. Even though the time signature may be $\frac{4}{4}$ or $\frac{3}{4}$, by adding syncopation it may be more difficult to feel the pulse naturally. Syncopation naturally creates more rhythmic drive and energy. It is used in jazz extensively.

There are countless ways to syncopate. Here are just a few examples of syncopation.

Swing

Swing Music vs. Swing Feel

Music that swings and Swing Music are not necessarily the same thing. Swing Music swings but not all jazz that **swings is Swing.**

The Swing Feel

The swing feel is written in $\frac{4}{4}$ time, but we feel the accents on beats 2 and 4. This syncopated rhythm helps to create the swing feel. However, there is a little more to it. The amount of time given to two notes, one after another, even though they are of equal value, is actually not equal in swing time. For example, two eighth notes would not be given the same amount of time. The first one would be given slightly more time, indicating a dotted eighth note, and yet it is not quite a dotted eighth note. The two notes are usually written as if they are of equal value but the feel would be indicated by the word "swing."

This swing feel is present in all styles of jazz; Ragtime, New Orleans, Dixieland, Chicago, Swing, Bebop, Cool/Hard Bop and even in free jazz. It is absolutely essential in jazz. After all, "It Don't Mean a Thing, If It Ain't Got That Swing!"

The Swing Style

Swing refers to the jazz style which occurred in the 1930s as jazz musicians moved from Chicago to New York City. Swing music was extremely popular and, simply put, made a person want to dance and move. It was performed at dance halls and, thanks to Benny Goodman, the "King of Swing" it was performed at venues such as Carnegie Hall. During this swing era, several big bands were developed such as Glenn Miller and the Dorsey Brothers, Ben Moten and Count Basie.

Swing Dance

At a place called The Savoy Ballroom in Harlem, New York City, Swing music and dance were inseparable. People went to the The Savoy in droves either to watch the dancers or to dance. As the Swing bands played, the dancers made up new steps just about every night. In 1935, a dancer named Frankie "Musclehead" Manning is credited with creating the first airsteps that lead to the birth of a dance called the Lindy Hop.

The Blues

Without the blues, we wouldn't have jazz. The blues originated many years ago but really began to take shape in the late 19th century. Filled with emotion, this rich form of music and storytelling began with the work songs of the African slaves. This music was an extension of their lives. They sang the Blues when they were sad, when they were happy, to make them feel better, and/or to tell a story.

The standard blues form is twelve bars. The standard blues chord progression is: I-IV-I-V-I. In musical terms these are known as the the tonic (I), subdominant (IV) and the dominant (V). Whether or not you consider yourself to be a *musician*, these three chords are fundamental in music and recognizable to most ears. Therefore the blues progression is easily identifiable for most people.

Standard Blues Form with Bass Note

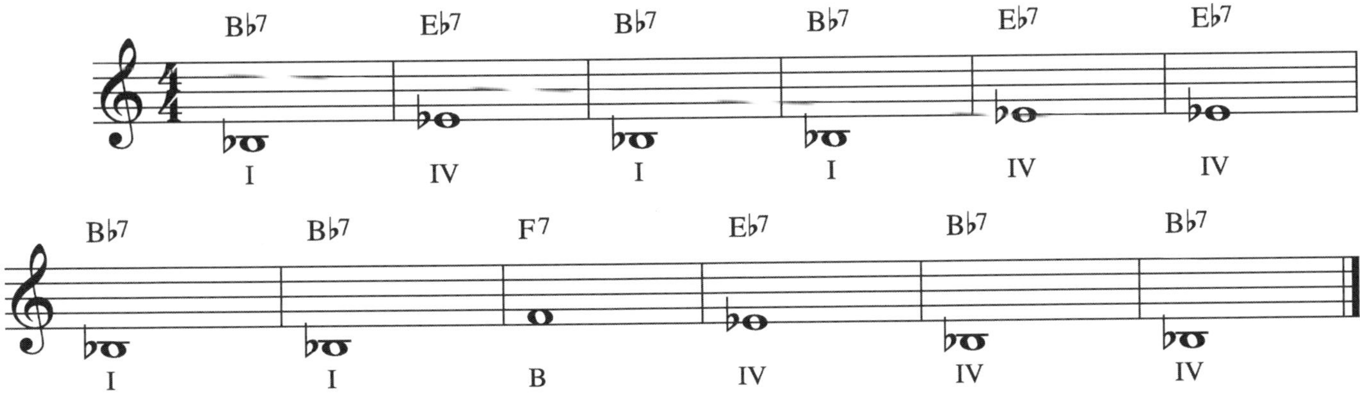

Variations on this form are common. Of course all variations are done so as not to disturb the basic nature and function of the Blues.

Ella Fitzgerald Listening List

- "How High the Moon": *The Very Best of Ella*
- "Stompin' at the Savoy": *The Best of Ella Fitzgerald and Louis Armstrong*
- "Take the A Train": *Ella Live*
- "A Tisket, A Tasket": *The Very Best of Ella*
- "Billie's Bounce": *Bluella*
- "Party Blues": *Count Basie and Joe Williams*
- "Fascinating Rhythm": *Ella Sings the George and Ira Gershwin Songbook*
- "Duke's Place": *Bluella*
- "Cheek to Cheek": *Ella and Louis*
- "I've Got My Love to Keep Me Warm": *Ella and Louis*
- "Moonlight in Vermont": *Ella and Louis*
- "Flying Home": *Heatwave*
- "It's Only a Paper Moon": *The Harold Arlen Songbook*

Miles Davis Listening List

- "So What": *Kind of Blue*
- "Freddie Freeloader": *Kind of Blue*
- "All Blues": *Kind of Blue*
- "Boplicity": *Birth of the Cool*
- "Move": *Birth of the Cool*
- "Someday My Prince Will Come": *Someday My Prince Will Come*
- "My Funny Valentine": *My Funny Valentine*

Louis Armstrong Listening List

- "West End Blues": *The Ultimate Collection or The Best of the Hot Fives and Hot Sevens Recordings*
- "The Blues Are Brewing": *Bluebird's Best – Louis Armstrong Sings and Swings*
- "Cornet Chop Suey": *Hot Fives and Sevens, Vol 1.*
- "What A Wonderful World"
- "Cottontail": *Duke Ellington and Louis Armstrong*
- "Hello Dolly": *20th Century Masters – The Millennium Collection – The Best of Louis Armstrong*
- "Heebie Jeebie": *The Complete Hot Five and Hot Seven Recordings, Vol. 1*
- "Basin Street Blues": *A Portrait of Louis Armstrong – The Birth of the All Stars*
- "When the Saints Go Marching In": *The Very Best of Louis*

Charlie Parker Listening List

- "Ornithology": *Charlie "Bird" Parker Ornithology*
- "Koko": *Diz n' Bird at Carnegie Hall*
- "Now's the Time": *Birdsong (with Miles Davis)*
- "Anthropology": *Summit Meeting at Birdland*
- "Billie's Bounce": *The Savoy Recordings*
- "Groovin' High": *Summit Meeting at Birdland*
- "Dewey Square": *The Dial Masters*
- "Donna Lee": *Chasin' the Bird*
- "My Little Suede Shoes": *Bird Gets the Worm*
- "Scrapple From the Apple": *April in Paris*
- "Yardbird Suite": *The Ultimate Collection*